BREAKTHROUGH BLENDING!

CREATIVE & DELICIOUS RECIPES FOR YOUR
NINJA™ KITCHEN SYSTEM

Pascoe Publishing, Inc.
Rocklin, California

Cover & Interior Design by KB Designs
Published in the United States of America by

Pascoe Publishing, Inc.
Rocklin, California
www. pascoepublishing. com

ISBN: 978-1-929862-92-4

Printed in China

TABLE OF CONTENTS

INTRODUCTION

Pack up and put away your food processor, juicer, heavy stand mixer and blender because your *Ninja™ Kitchen System* has arrived! Food prep has never been so easy: create frosty cold resort-style cocktails, enticing appetizer dips and spreads, healthful smoothies, whole-fruit juices, sauces, soups, salsas, and much, much more!

To help get you started, we've included in this cookbook a wide variety of recipes for every day – entrées, desserts, salads, bakery goods and snacks. Each has easy-to-follow techniques and is crafted to delight your family and friends with exceptional flavors.

Once you try these recipes, you'll be well on your way to creating your own favorite juices, smoothies, snacks and more. Here's to you and your own delicious and delightful *Ninja™ Kitchen System* experiences!

— Deb Roussou & Connie Neckels

SECRETS TO SUCCESS
WITH YOUR NINJA™ KITCHEN SYSTEM

DURING THE PROCESS of creating these recipes, we've discovered some short-cuts and secrets to recipe success. We like to share them with you:

• The results of your recipe will depend on how well you measure the ingredients. Using dry and fluid measuring cups when needed and measuring with measuring spoons (instead of that random spoon out of your drawer) will guarantee a success.

• The unique Ninja™ Kitchen System blades are designed to be removed before pouring or spooning out ingredients. We love this feature!

• When a recipe calls for more than 1 cup of flour, add the first cup and blend briefly. Continue adding flour 1 cup at a time to ensure that the dough or batter evenly absorbs the flour. Turn off the Ninja™ Kitchen System and clean the sides of the pitcher as needed.

• Select speed ❶ whenever you use the dough hook or dough paddle. Speed ❶ is perfect for the gradual incorporation of ingredients in batters and doughs. Do not use speed ❷ or ❸ while using the dough hook or dough paddle.

• It's a toss-up whether or not to strain fruit and vegetable juices before drinking them. Use a fine sieve for straining if beverages seem too thick, or strain half the juice and leave the rest intact and then blend together.

• As tempting as it may be to rush through your prep time, don't overfill the Pitchers or Single Serve Cup with liquid; use the maximum fill line as your absolute guide.

• Avoid any splatters by covering the pour spout with a small towel as you add ingredients while the system is turned on.

SWEET
STRAWBERRY
SMOOTHIE
P. 18

SPARKLING LEMONADE WITH FRESH BASIL

Serves 6 to 8

Perfect for a kitchen full of thirsty kids!

3 FRESH LEMONS, PEELED, SEEDED AND CUT INTO CHUNKS
6 OUNCE CAN FROZEN LEMONADE CONCENTRATE, UNDILUTED
28 OUNCES CLUB SODA
1 LITER GINGER ALE
FRESH BASIL SPRIGS FOR GARNISH

Place the lemons, lemonade concentrate and 2 cups of the club soda into the 72 oz. Pitcher. Blend on ② until smooth. Strain the juice through a fine sieve. Pour the juice into a large pitcher and add the remaining club soda and ginger ale. Stir well to combine. Pour the juice over ice and garnish each serving with basil.

Tip
Freeze fresh strawberries and float a few in each glass as a garnish.

APPLE, CARROT & GINGER TEA

Serves 2

The tart-sweet combinations in this tea are smooth and refreshing. Fresh ginger can be overwhelming, so start with just a little and add more as you prefer.

1 SMALL GREEN APPLE, PEELED, CORED AND CHUNKED
1 CARROT PEELED AND CUT INTO CHUNKS
2 CUPS PREPARED ICED TEA
1 TEASPOON SUGAR
PINCH FRESH GINGER, GRATED

Place the apple and carrot into a microwave-safe bowl and add ¼ cup water. Microwave on High for 3 to 5 minutes, or until the apple and carrot are soft. Cool completely, then spoon the apple, carrot and juices into the 72 oz. Pitcher and add the remaining ingredients. Blend on ❸ until smooth. Remove and strain the tea through a fine sieve. Pour the tea over ice cubes into tall glasses and serve at once.

✳ Tip

Fresh ginger has been used for centuries in China, where it is prized for both its flavor and the soothing effect it has on the digestive system.

APPLE & PINEAPPLE JUICE BLEND

Makes about 6 cups of juice blend

Cooking the apples first allows the fruit flavor to mellow and sweeten naturally.

4 COOKING APPLES, PEELED AND CORED
½ CUP FRESH PINEAPPLE, CUT IN CHUNKS
½ TEASPOON GROUND CINNAMON
4 CUPS APPLE JUICE

Place the apples and the pineapple in a microwave-safe bowl and add 2 tablespoons of water. Cover with plastic wrap and cook on High for 6 minutes, or until very tender. Let cool completely, then spoon the mixture into the 72 oz. Pitcher and add the cinnamon.

Blend the mixture on ② until smooth. Depending on your preference, pour the mixture through a fine sieve and add to the apple juice, or combine the apple/pineapple mixture with the juice and serve as is. Refrigerate any leftover juice.

✳ Tip

If you like the fresh flavor of a homemade applesauce, change up this recipe by omitting the apple juice while blending. The results will be a sweet and sassy apple-pineapple sauce!

FRESH PEAR & MANGO NECTAR

Serves 4 to 6

Pears and mangos blend into an incredibly fresh-tasting and lightly sweet juice. Place your ripe pears in the refrigerator until use so that the juice will be clear instead of cloudy.

6 RIPE PEARS, CORED AND CUT INTO LARGE PIECES
4 CUPS MANGO NECTAR

Place the pears in a large microwave-safe bowl and add 2 tablespoons of water. Cook on High for 3 to 4 minutes, or until very tender. Remove and cool slightly.

Place half of the pears and nectar into the 72 oz. Pitcher and blend on ❷ until uniformly smooth. Strain the juice through a fine sieve and pour into a large container or pitcher. Repeat with the remaining nectar and pears. Serve over ice or chill until ready to serve.

Tip

Look for mango nectar sold in cans in the juice or health food aisle of your grocery store.

PINEAPPLE BANANA SWIRL
Serves 2

Start with pineapples and bananas; then add any other fruit you have on hand. Be ready to share this wonderfully fresh juice!

2 CUPS FRESH PINEAPPLE, CUT INTO PIECES
1 BANANA, PEELED, CUT IN HALF
2 CUPS PINEAPPLE JUICE

Place all ingredients in the 72 oz. Pitcher. Blend on ③ for 20 seconds, or until smooth. Remove and serve or, if desired, strain through a fine sieve before serving.

Tip
Add strawberries, raspberries, boysenberries or blueberries for a seasonal treat!

ORANGE DOUBLE-UP

Serves 4 to 6

Packed with vitamin C, this juice will be as tart and as sweet as the oranges you choose.

4 CUPS ORANGE JUICE, DIVIDED
½ CUP FROZEN ORANGE JUICE CONCENTRATE
2 MEDIUM FRESH ORANGES, PEELED, SEEDED AND CUT INTO PIECES
16 OUNCES CARBONATED WATER

Pour 2 cups of orange juice into the 72 oz. Pitcher. Add the juice concentrate and the fresh oranges. Blend on ❷ until uniformly smooth. Pour the mixture into a large serving pitcher and add the remaining orange juice and carbonated water. Stir well to blend. Pour over ice and serve.

Tip

This bubbly juice blend can serve as a special breakfast or brunch drink for kids in lieu of champagne punch or mimosas. Serve in plastic champagne flutes for even more flair!

MANGO, PAPAYA & BANANA NECTAR

Serves 2 to 3

This gentle reminder of the tropics is a delicious break from typical juice blends.

½ CUP RIPE MANGO, CUT INTO CHUNKS
½ CUP RIPE PAPAYA, CUT INTO SLICES
½ RIPE BANANA, CUT INTO CHUNKS
16 OUNCES GUAVA NECTAR

Place the fruit in the 72 oz. Pitcher and add the nectar. Blend on ② until smooth. Pour into small glasses and serve right away.

Tip
Double this recipe easily for a crowd-pleasing juice blend!

BREAKFAST VEGGIE BLEND

Serves 1

A powerful antioxidant breakfast blend!

1 CUP VEGETABLE BLEND JUICE
¼ CUP FRESH CARROT, CUT INTO CHUNKS
8 LEAVES FRESH SPINACH, TORN
PINCH SALT
PINCH BLACK PEPPER

Place all of the ingredients in the Single Serve Cup and press the Single Serve button until smooth.

⁎Tip
For extra protein power, add up to ½ cup packed spinach leaves. You'll have energy for the whole day!

SWEET STRAWBERRY SMOOTHIE
Serves 2 to 3

This recipe invites you to add a little bit of cream to your strawberries, so why not add some rich decadence to your day?

½ CUP HALF-AND-HALF CREAM
½ CUP WHOLE MILK
1 CUP RIPE, SWEET STRAWBERRIES, STEMMED AND WASHED
½ CUP LOWFAT VANILLA-FLAVORED YOGURT
2 CUPS ICE CUBES

Pour the cream and milk into the 72 oz. Pitcher and add the strawberries, yogurt and ice cubes. Blend on ③ until the mixture is very smooth and no fruit pieces remain. Pour into glasses and serve right away.

Tip
This smoothie is a perfect "starter" recipe if you've never before tried making your own smoothie. Change it by adding different seasonal fruits and other flavored yogurts.

BANANA PINEAPPLE SMOOTHIE
Serves 3 to 4

Just a hint of coconut plays against the tart pineapple and smooth banana flavors.

2 CUPS PINEAPPLE JUICE
1 CUP PINEAPPLE CHUNKS, FRESH OR CANNED
1 SMALL RIPE BANANA, CUT INTO CHUNKS
¼ CUP UNSWEETENED COCONUT MILK
1 TABLESPOON HONEY
3 CUPS ICE CUBES

Pour the juice into the 72 oz. Pitcher and add the pineapple, banana, coconut milk, honey and ice. Blend on ③ until very smooth. Pour into glasses and serve at once.

Tip
If you can't find unsweetened coconut milk, substitute sweetened milk and omit the honey.

TRIPLE BERRY TWIST
Serves 3 to 4

Substitute any fresh, ripe berries…and create a new twist of your own.

½ CUP FRESH, RIPE RASPBERRIES
½ CUP FRESH, RIPE BLACKBERRIES
½ CUP FRESH, RIPE STRAWBERRIES
½ CUP FAT-FREE, NON-DAIRY VANILLA COFFEE CREAMER
½ CUP LOWFAT OR NONFAT MILK
1 TABLESPOON SUGAR OR SUGAR SUBSTITUTE
3 CUPS ICE CUBES

Place the fruit in the 72 oz. Pitcher and add the creamer, milk and sugar. Add the ice cubes and blend on ❸ until completely smooth. Serve right away.

Tip
This recipe is perfect if you are watching your fat and calorie counts!

SUMMER SWEET PEACH SMOOTHIE
Serves 2 to 3

There's really no substitute for fresh peaches in this smoothie so make this when the peach trees are hanging heavy with their luscious fruit. Use very ripe, soft peaches and add a bit of ground ginger if you're feeling adventurous.

2 RIPE, SWEET PEACHES, PITTED AND PEELED
1 CUP LOWFAT PEACH-FLAVORED YOGURT
1 CUP PEACH NECTAR, CHILLED
2½ CUPS ICE CUBES

Place all ingredients into the 72 oz. Pitcher. Blend on ❸ until completely smooth. Pour into glasses and serve right away.

Tip

Chill a travel mug in your freezer and pour your smoothie into the mug before your commute to work in the morning. The mug will keep your smoothie frosty cold for many miles!

HOT CRANBERRY SOOTHER
Serves 4

A tasty relief when coffee and tea become tiresome.

½ CUP CANNED CRANBERRY JELLY
4 CUPS CRANBERRY JUICE COCKTAIL
1 RIPE ORANGE, PEELED AND SEEDED, CUT INTO CHUNKS
PINCH GROUND CINNAMON
PINCH GROUND CLOVES

Spoon the cranberry jelly into the 72 oz. Pitcher and add the juice and orange pieces. Blend on ③ until smooth. If desired, strain the mixture through a fine sieve.

Pour the mixture into a saucepan and add the cinnamon and cloves. Heat until warmed through. Ladle into mugs and serve.

Tip
We think of this tart and sweet hot drink as soon as the nights start to turn crisp and cold and frost is on the roof in the morning.

TANGERINE TANGO
Serves 4 to 6

Add a shot of dark rum as a sure remedy against a freezing winter's evening.

3 RIPE TANGERINES OR MANDARIN ORANGES, PEELED AND SEEDED
1 RIPE TANGERINE (OR MANDARIN), PEELED AND THINLY SLICED
8 CUPS APPLE JUICE, DIVIDED
1 TABLESPOON DARK BROWN SUGAR

Place the 3 tangerines in the 72 oz. Pitcher and add 2 cups of the apple juice. Blend on ③ until the fruit is uniform. Strain the juice through a fine sieve.

In a medium saucepan, heat the blended tangerine and apple juice, remaining apple juice and sugar until steaming. Stir occasionally. Place one slice of tangerine in the bottom of individual mugs and ladle the hot juice over the slices. Serve while hot.

Tip
Use very ripe tangerines or mandarin oranges for the best burst of flavor in this special drink.

HOT CHAI TEA
Serves 2

This is a mix of the traditional and the new chai tea methods of preparation. Don't skimp on the spices; when crushed, they add a tremendous boost of flavor.

2 CUPS HALF AND HALF CREAM
¼ INCH PIECE FRESH GINGER, PEELED
¼ TEASPOON GROUND CINNAMON
1 POD CARDAMOM
1 TEASPOON SUGAR
2 CUPS WATER
2 TABLESPOONS BLACK TEA, LOOSE OR IN BAG

Place the cream, ginger, cinnamon and cardamom in the 72 oz. Pitcher. Blend on ❶ for 20 seconds. Add the sugar and water and blend again for 10 seconds. Pour the tea into a medium saucepan and heat until the liquid begins to bubble around the edges. Continue heating on a low simmer for 2 minutes, stirring occasionally. Remove from the heat and immediately add the black tea and let stand for 1 minute. Strain through a fine sieve and serve right away.

Tip

Don't bother paying high coffeehouse prices for this delicate tea. It only takes a few minutes to prepare in your *Ninja™ Kitchen System* and the process of simmering the tea over low heat is calming in itself.

ORANGE RUSSIAN TEA

Serves 1

Try this soothing tea whenever you have a sore throat or cold – it's practically medicinal.

1 CUP WATER
1 TEASPOON INSTANT UNSWEETENED ICED TEA
1 CUP ORANGE JUICE
1 TEASPOON WHOLE CLOVES
½ INCH PIECE WHOLE CINNAMON
1 POD CARDAMOM

Place all ingredients into the 40 oz. Pitcher. Blend on ❸ for 20 seconds. Strain the tea through a fine sieve. Microwave or heat in a saucepan on the stove until steaming.

Tip

Make this for a crowd by adjusting the ingredient amounts and add a shot of honey-based Canadian whiskey (such as Yukon Jack™) per serving for a kick of warmth!

FROSTY
ORANGE CREAM
P. 32

CHAPTER TWO

FROZEN DRINK SPECIALTIES

MOCHA FREEZE
Serves 4

Keeping instant cocoa and coffee in your pantry ensures that you'll always have the ingredients for this delicious frozen drink at hand.

⅓ CUP INSTANT COCOA MIX
2 TABLESPOONS INSTANT COFFEE
¼ CUP SUGAR
¼ CUP HOT WATER
1 QUART LOWFAT MILK, PARTIALLY FROZEN UNTIL CHUNKY

In a small bowl, mix together the cocoa mix, coffee and sugar. Add the hot water and stir to blend well.

Pour the mixture into the 72 oz. pitcher. Add the partially frozen milk to the pitcher. Blend on ③ until very smooth. Pour into 4 glasses and serve at once.

Tip

The partially frozen milk used in this recipe takes the place of ice cubes. You can easily add protein and calcium to your diet by interchanging frozen milk for any recipes that call for ice cubes. You'll get the same smooth and icy results.

BLAST O' BERRIES SHAKE
Serves 3 to 4

Caramelized strawberries provide the naturally sweet and fruity flavor for this shake.

1 TABLESPOON BUTTER
2 CUPS STRAWBERRIES, CLEANED AND HULLED, SLICED
¼ CUP LOWFAT MILK
1 TEASPOON PURE VANILLA EXTRACT
4 CUPS PREMIUM VANILLA ICE CREAM

Place the butter in a saucepan and add the strawberries. Heat over medium-low, stirring occasionally, for 5 minutes, to caramelize the fruit. Do not allow the fruit to brown or burn. Remove from the heat and let cool.

Place the cooled strawberries, milk and vanilla in the 72 oz. Pitcher. Blend on ❶ until smooth. Add the ice cream and blend on ❸ until smooth. Spoon into glasses and serve right away.

✳ Tip
Try this with caramelized blackberries, boysenberries or raspberries as well.

MOCHA AT MIDNIGHT SHAKE
Serves 2 (large) or 4 (small)

The perfect answer to a midnight raid on the freezer.

¼ CUP HALF AND HALF CREAM
¼ CUP COLD PREPARED COFFEE
¼ CUP PREPARED HOT FUDGE TOPPING
3½ CUPS PREMIUM CHOCOLATE ICE CREAM

Pour the cream and coffee into the 72 oz. Pitcher. Blend on ① for a few seconds. Add the fudge topping and the ice cream. Blend on ③ until smooth and frosty. Pour or spoon into glasses and serve right away.

❋ Tip

It's easy to create a "lighter" version of this decadent shake – use lowfat milk, chocolate syrup and chocolate frozen yogurt to cut the calories and fat in half.

CARAMEL CRÈME PARFAITS
Serves 4

Silky, rich caramel and ice cream partner with a twist of granola for crunchy goodness!

4 CUPS PREMIUM VANILLA ICE CREAM
½ CUP PREMIUM CARAMEL SAUCE, DIVIDED
½ CUP LOWFAT MILK
1½ CUPS CRUNCHY GRANOLA MIX

Place the ice cream and ¼ cup of caramel sauce into the 72 oz. Pitcher. Add the milk and blend on ❸ until very smooth. Remove and assemble the parfaits. Drizzle a small amount of the remaining caramel sauce down the sides of 4 glasses. Layer the ice cream and crunchy granola into each glass. Top each parfait with a drizzle of the remaining caramel sauce and serve at once.

Tip
Add layers of sweet sliced strawberries to each parfait for a sweet and healthful delight.

FROSTY ORANGE CREAM
Serves 2 to 3

Cold, tart and creamy!

12 OUNCES LOWFAT MILK, CHILLED
¼ CUP FROZEN ORANGE JUICE CONCENTRATE
1 TEASPOON VANILLA EXTRACT
2 TABLESPOONS SUGAR
3 CUPS ICE CUBES

Pour the milk into the 72 oz. Pitcher and add the orange juice concentrate, vanilla and sugar. Blend on ❶ for a few seconds. Add the ice cubes and blend on ❸ until frosty and smooth. Pour into glasses and serve right away.

Tip

This recipe is a variation of a well-known orange cream drink and it captures that same delicious fruit and cream flavor tango. We did not add egg to froth this as is commonly included, but you can always add one egg for extra energy and protein.

SOY LATTE FREEZE
Serves 3 to 4

A nice change of pace from the typical coffeehouse drink.

¾ CUP VANILLA-FLAVORED SOYMILK (REGULAR OR LIGHT)
2 SHOTS ESPRESSO COFFEE, AT ROOM TEMPERATURE
1 TABLESPOON SUGAR
3 CUPS ICE CUBES

Pour the soymilk and coffee into the 72 oz. Pitcher. Add the sugar and blend for a few seconds. Add the ice cubes and blend on ❸ until very smooth. Pour into glasses and serve right away.

*Tip

Change it up to almond milk or nonfat dairy creamer in place of the soymilk. Each little change results in refreshing, new flavors.

DUO DARK CHOCOLATE FRAPPE
Serves 4

Decadently rich, but decidedly easy.

½ CUP DARK CHOCOLATE FUDGE SAUCE
½ CUP CHOCOLATE MILK
1 CUP ICE CUBES
3 CUPS PREMIUM FUDGE ICE CREAM

Prepare 4 tall glasses by pouring the fudge sauce in ribbons down the sides of each glass. Set aside.

Pour the milk into the 72 oz. Pitcher and add the ice cubes. Blend on ③ until smooth. Add the fudge ice cream and blend again on ③. Use a spatula to clean the sides of the pitcher, if needed, and blend again on ③ until completely smooth.

Pour the frappe into each prepared glass and serve at once.

✳ Tip

Half the fun of this recipe is seeing the rich chocolate ribbons running down the sides of the glasses. Use the fanciest glassware you have or try champagne flutes or even stemmed wineglasses.

ICED TROPICAL RAINBOW
Makes 4 small servings

Your *Ninja™ Kitchen System* will perfectly turn ice cubes into snowy-white ice powder. Top off with flavors of your choice for a tropical blast!

4 CUPS ICE CUBES
3 FLAVORED SYRUPS (SUCH AS TORANI®)
(WE SUGGEST: BLUE RASPBERRY, PINEAPPLE, AND MANGO)

Place the ice cubes in the 72 oz. Pitcher and blend on ③ until a very uniform powder is formed. Using a large spoon, lightly pack the ice powder into 4 small cups or glasses. Pour 1 ounce each of three different flavored syrups over the top of each serving. Serve at once.

Tip
Keep several flavored syrups on hand in your pantry for the hottest summer days when your kids will appreciate this icy treat. If you want to really impress your kids, serve in classic white paper cone cups, available at kitchen supply stores.

PINEAPPLE & MANGO FROSTEE
Serves 2 to 3

This frozen drink has an added boost of nutritional value with fresh fruit and calcium. Enjoy!

1 CUP FRESH PINEAPPLE, CUT IN LARGE PIECES
1 CUP MANGO, CUT INTO LARGE PIECES
½ CUP LOWFAT MILK
1 TEASPOON HONEY
1 PINT MANGO SORBET

Place the pineapple and mango in the 72 oz. Pitcher and add the milk. Blend on ② for about 10 seconds, or until smooth. Add the honey and sorbet and blend on ③ until smooth. Pour into 2 glasses and serve at once.

✳ Tip

Use any kind of sorbet you have on hand – pineapple, orange, raspberry – everything works in this luscious recipe!

CHOCOLATE MINT CHIP MILKSHAKE

Serves 3

Thick and rich – a classic milkshake in a minute.

½ CUP SEMI-SWEET CHOCOLATE CHIP PIECES
4 CUPS MINT ICE CREAM
½ CUP LOWFAT MILK
MINT LEAVES FOR GARNISH

Place the chocolate chip pieces in the 72 oz. Pitcher and blend on ① for a few seconds until the chips are uniformly chopped. Add the ice cream and milk and blend on ③ until smooth.

Pour or spoon the milkshake into tall glasses and garnish each glass with mint leaves before serving.

Tip

Toss white or milk chocolate chips in just about any dessert drink for a sweet change.

FROZEN CHOCOLATE CHEESECAKE
Serves 4

Classic chocolate cheesecake – in an ice-cold drink.

¼ CUP WHOLE MILK
½ CUP CREAM CHEESE (WHIPPED OR REGULAR)
3½ CUPS PREMIUM CHOCOLATE ICE CREAM
¼ CUP RASPBERRY JAM
½ CUP PREPARED LOWFAT WHIPPED TOPPING

Pour the milk into the 72 oz. Pitcher and add the cream cheese. Pulse for a few seconds to blend. Add the chocolate ice cream and blend on ③ until very smooth. Spoon the mixture into 4 small glasses.

Top each shake with a dollop of raspberry jam and the prepared whipped topping. Serve at once.

Tip

Substitute lowfat cream cheese, lowfat chocolate frozen yogurt, lowfat milk and light cream if you want to cut about fifty percent of the calories and fat – without losing the luscious flavor – in this easy recipe.

CANDY BAR CRUNCH

Serves 4

Seems like a match made in heaven – crunchy chocolate candy and sweet vanilla ice cream!

3 LARGE CHOCOLATE CANDY BARS WITH ALMONDS OR PEANUTS
3½ CUPS PREMIUM VANILLA OR CHOCOLATE ICE CREAM
½ CUP MILK
SLIVERED ALMONDS OR CHOPPED PEANUTS FOR GARNISH

Place the candy bars in the 72 oz. Pitcher and add the ice cream and milk. Blend on ③ until the candy is uniformly chopped and the drink is smooth. Spoon into glasses and garnish each serving with nuts, if preferred.

Tip

The list of candy bars to use in this recipe is endless. Try any chocolate/nut combinations or look for nougat/nut bars and toffee/nut specialties. The *Ninja™ Kitchen System* will smoothly blend your favorite flavors.

ROCKY ROAD SHAKE

Serves 4

Make any number of substitutions in this recipe to create your own favorite. Try swapping the nuts or ice cream flavors, or add candied or dried fruit.

½ CUP LOWFAT MILK
4 CUPS PREMIUM CHOCOLATE ICE CREAM
1 CUP MINIATURE MARSHMALLOWS
¼ CUP MARASCHINO CHERRIES, PITTED, STEMS REMOVED
¼ CUP WALNUTS, HALVED

Pour the milk into the 72 oz. Pitcher and add the ice cream. Add the marshmallows, cherries and walnuts. Blend on ③ for about 20 seconds, or until the ingredients are uniformly chopped and the drink is fairly smooth.

Spoon into glasses and serve at once.

Tip

Rocky road ice cream used to be a staple at the corner drug store and, although tastes have become more sophisticated these days, there is still something very satisfying about the taste of nuts mixed with sweet cherries and marshmallows wrapped up in melty ice cream.

PURE VANILLA MALT

Serves 2

Simply perfection – without any other ingredients!

½ CUP LOWFAT MILK
3 CUPS PREMIUM VANILLA ICE CREAM
¼ CUP MALTED MILK POWDER
½ TEASPOON VANILLA EXTRACT

Pour the milk into the 72 oz. Pitcher and add the ice cream, malted milk powder and vanilla extract. Blend on ❸ until smooth and creamy. Pour into 2 large glasses and serve at once.

Tip

Use this simple recipe as the starting place for all your favorite additions – think fresh fruit, nuts, dark chocolate, butterscotch, specialty candies, sandwich cookies, and more. Toss in chocolate malt balls, too!

ESPRESSO ICE CREAM FREEZE

Serves 3 to 4

This frozen drink salutes coffee in three perfect ways – espresso coffee, coffee beans, and coffee ice cream.

2 SHOTS ESPRESSO COFFEE, AT ROOM TEMPERATURE
¼ CUP CHOCOLATE-COVERED ESPRESSO BEANS
¼ CUP MILK
4 CUPS PREMIUM COFFEE ICE CREAM

Pour the coffee into the 72 oz. Pitcher and add the espresso beans. Blend on ❷ until the beans are uniformly chopped. Add the milk and ice cream and blend on ❸ until thick and smooth. Spoon into tall glass mugs and serve right away.

FROZEN
BLUE BAYOU
P. 46

CHAPTER THREE

COCKTAILS & PARTY DRINKS

FROZEN BLUE BAYOU
Makes 4 to 6 servings

This cool refresher is made with Blue Curacao, an orange flavored liqueur that originated in the Caribbean. It is now produced mainly in France and is available in many colors.

4 CUPS ICE CUBES, CRUSHED
6 OUNCES GOOD QUALITY VODKA
4 OUNCES BLUE CURACAO
2 CUPS LEMONADE
4 TO 6 FROZEN LIME WEDGES FOR GARNISH

Place the ice into the 72 oz. Pitcher and add the remaining ingredients, except the lime wedges. Blend on ❸ until smooth. Pour into tall chilled glasses and garnish with lime wedges.

✳ Tip

Invest in a bottle of Blue Curacao, which is reasonably priced, for a splash of color and flavor at your next party. The vivid blue color alone invites a happy response from each guest!

THE PERFECT BLENDED MARGARITA
Makes 4 servings

It's hard to make a mistake when using a can to measure the ingredients; clever and very, very good!

12 OUNCE CAN FROZEN LIMEADE
1 CAN GOOD QUALITY TEQUILA
⅓ CAN TRIPLE SEC
½ CAN FRESH LIME JUICE
½ CAN WATER
4 CUPS CRUSHED ICE CUBES

GARNISH
½ CUP COARSE SALT FOR GARNISH
4 LIME SLICES FOR GARNISH

Place all ingredients into 72 oz. Pitcher and blend on ❸ until smooth. Pour the salt onto a shallow saucer. Moisten the rim of each margarita glass with lime juice, then dip the rim of the glass in the salt. Fill prepared glasses with the blended margarita and garnish with a slice of lime.

Tip

Don't skimp on the special touches, such as coarse salt and slices of lime. The little garnishes make all the difference in this popular drink.

THE PERFECT TOP-SHELF MARGARITA ON THE ROCKS

Makes 4 servings

The higher the quality of the alcohol, the higher shelf it occupies in many fine bars. This recipe calls for top quality alcohol, hence the name, Top-Shelf Margarita.

12 OUNCES GOOD QUALITY SILVER TEQUILA
4 OUNCES ORANGE FLAVORED LIQUEUR
(COINTREAU OR GRAND MARNIER)
8 OUNCES FRESH LIME JUICE
4 CUPS CRUSHED ICE CUBES

GARNISH
½ CUP COARSE SALT FOR GARNISH
4 LIME SLICES

Pour tequila, Cointreau and fresh lime juice into the 72 oz. Pitcher and blend on ① until well-blended. Sprinkle the salt onto a shallow saucer. Moisten the rim of each margarita glass with the lime juice, then dip the rim of the glass in the salt. Add crushed ice cubes to prepared glasses and fill with the margarita. Garnish with a slice of lime.

Tip

Whether you are an "On the Rocks" purist or you love a smooth, frosty blended margarita, adding a float of Cointreau or Grand Marnier on top creates a lasting impression. Your guests will definitely be back for more.

FRESH COCONUT PINA COLADA

Makes 2 servings

The ultimate tropical vacation cocktail.

2 CUPS CRUSHED ICE CUBES
4 OUNCES LIGHT RUM
2 OUNCES DARK RUM
¾ CUP PINEAPPLE JUICE
4 OUNCES COCONUT MILK
SHAVED FRESH COCONUT FOR GARNISH

Place the ice into the 72 oz. Pitcher and add the remaining ingredients, except the garnish. Blend on ③ until smooth.

Pour into chilled glasses and garnish with the shaved fresh coconut. Serve with a straw.

Tip

If you want to impress, serve with fresh pineapple spears dipped in milk chocolate. Wow!

FROZEN WHITE SANGRIA

Makes 6 servings

To make this cool Spanish cocktail, you need to start the day before, as the fresh pineapple and oranges must be frozen.

1 CUP CRUSHED ICE CUBES

2 CUPS FRESH PINEAPPLE, CHOPPED, FROZEN

2 LARGE ORANGES PEELED AND SECTIONED, FROZEN

2 CUPS DRY WHITE WINE, CHILLED

½ CUP BRANDY

½ CUP ORANGE FLAVORED LIQUEUR (TRIPLE SEC OR GRAND MARNIER)

6 MINT SPRIGS FOR GARNISH

Place the chopped pineapple and orange on a baking sheet and freeze until firm, at least 12 hours.

Place the frozen fruit and the remaining ingredients, except the garnish, into the 72 oz. Pitcher and blend on ③ until smooth. Pour into individual glasses and garnish each with mint.

Tip

Perfect for your next girls-night-out party! The frozen fruit really comes alive when blended with white wine, but the flavors are smooth. Double the recipe and use frozen fruit to float as garnishes.

STRAWBERRY DAIQUIRI

Makes 6 servings

As versatile as it is good, it's easy to substitute peaches, bananas, or your favorite fruit in this inviting drink.

8 OUNCES LIGHT RUM

4 OUNCES FRESH LIME JUICE

2 TABLESPOONS SUPERFINE SUGAR

2 CUPS HULLED FRESH STRAWBERRIES

4 OUNCES ORANGE FLAVORED LIQUEUR (TRIPLE SEC, COINTREAU OR GRAND MARNIER)

4 CUPS CRUSHED ICE CUBES

GARNISH

6 WHOLE STRAWBERRIES, HALVED

2 KIWI, PEELED AND CUT INTO 12 PIECES

6 MINT SPRIGS

6 THIN WOODEN SKEWERS

Place the rum, juice, sugar, strawberries and triple sec in the 72 oz. Pitcher and blend on ❷ until smooth. Add the ice cubes and blend again on ❸ until very smooth.

Thread the strawberries and kiwi alternately onto skewers. Divide the daiquiris into 6 chilled glasses and garnish with fruit skewers and mint.

Tip

When entertaining kids, omit the rum and orange-flavored liqueur and substitute 8 ounces of lemon-lime soda and 1 tablespoon of rum flavoring instead. Garnish with the fruit skewers for an added splash.

SEA BREEZE SOOTHER

Makes 4 servings

To create a Hawaiian Sea Breeze, replace the grapefruit juice with pineapple juice.

1 CUP GOOD QUALITY VODKA
1½ CUPS CRANBERRY JUICE
1½ CUPS GRAPEFRUIT JUICE
4 CUPS CRUSHED ICE CUBES
4 LIME SLICES FOR GARNISH

Pour the vodka, cranberry juice and grapefruit juice into the 72 oz. Pitcher and blend on ① until mixed and frothy.

Place the ice in chilled glasses, fill each with the drink and garnish with the lime slices.

Tip

This is the perfect cocktail for those who prefer tart and tangy over sweet. Serve with southwestern foods or whole grain crackers and a cheese spread. The full flavor of this drink can accompany hearty foods without becoming overwhelmed.

PINEAPPLE MANGO MOJITO
Makes 4 servings

It's hard to make a classic Mojito more tropical than it already is, but this really does the trick.

1 CUP FRESH PINEAPPLE CHUNKS
1 CUP FRESH MANGO CHUNKS
¼ CUP FRESH LIME JUICE
2 TABLESPOONS SUPER-FINE SUGAR
10 TO 12 MINT LEAVES
6 OUNCES LIGHT RUM
2 CUPS SPARKLING WATER
4 CUPS ICE CUBES

GARNISH
¼ CUP SUPERFINE SUGAR
4 LIME SLICES
4 SPRIGS OF MINT

Place the pineapple, mango, lime juice, sugar and mint into the 72 oz. Pitcher and blend on ❷ until smooth. Add the rum and 2 cups sparkling water and pulse until just blended.

Sprinkle the sugar onto a shallow saucer. Moisten the rim of each glass with lime and dip the rim of the glass into the sugar. Add the ice to the prepared glasses and fill each with the Pineapple Mango Mojito. Garnish with lime slices and a sprig of mint.

LEMON MERINGUE
Makes 2 servings

A fun twist on a Limoncello Martini.

3 OUNCES GOOD QUALITY CITRUS VODKA
2 OUNCES LIMONCELLO
1 OUNCE LIGHT CRÈME DE CACAO

Place all ingredients into the 72 oz. Pitcher and blend on ① until smooth. Pour into chilled martini glasses and serve.

Tip

Double or triple this recipe easily for a crowd and add mint for a garnish. This cocktail is especially good when the heat of the day hits the triple digits and then starts to cool in the evening.

FROZEN CUBAN MOJITO

Makes 2 servings

This minty refresher will have you dreaming of Old Havana.

¼ CUP SIMPLE SYRUP (RECIPE FOLLOWS)
¼ CUP FRESH LIME JUICE
10 FRESH MINT LEAVES
6 OUNCES LIGHT RUM
3 CUPS CRUSHED ICE CUBES
2 MINT SPRIGS FOR GARNISH

SIMPLE SYRUP
½ CUP WATER
½ CUP SUGAR

Place the simple syrup, lime juice and mint leaves into the 72 oz. Pitcher and blend on ① until combined. Add the rum and crushed ice and blend on ③ until smooth. Pour into rocks glasses and garnish with mint sprigs.

Simple Syrup: Combine water and sugar in a small sauce pan and bring to a boil. Simmer, while stirring, over low heat until the sugar dissolves. Cool to room temperature. Store in the refrigerator in a glass bottle.

MILK CHOCOLATE MUDSLIDE
Makes 4 servings

Can you say "Dessert?" These chocolate milkshakes are the ultimate treat!

4 OUNCES KAHLUA
4 OUNCES FRANGELICO
4 OUNCES GOOD QUALITY VODKA
4 LARGE SCOOPS CHOCOLATE ICE CREAM
2 CUPS CRUSHED ICE CUBES

GARNISH
¼ CUP SUPERFINE SUGAR
2 TABLESPOONS POWDERED COCOA
4 CHOCOLATE ROLLED WAFERS

Place all ingredients, except the garnishes, into the 72 oz. Pitcher and blend on ❸ until smooth.

In a small bowl, blend the superfine sugar and cocoa in a shallow saucer. Moisten the rim of each glass with Kahlua and dip the rim into the sugar cocoa mixture. Fill each glass with the drink and garnish with a rolled wafer.

Tip
Substitute thin mint candy sticks as a garnish in this easy frozen cocktail.

ITALIAN BELLINI

Makes 4 servings

The Bellini was invented in 1948 at Harry's Bar in Venice, Italy, a known hang-out of writer Ernest Hemingway.

6 MEDIUM WHITE PEACHES, PITTED AND PEELED
1 BOTTLE ITALIAN SPARKLING WINE, CHILLED
(RECOMMEND PROSECCO)
4 SPLASHES CRÈME DE FRAMBOISE

Place the peaches into the 72 oz. Pitcher and blend on ❸ until uniformly smooth. Spoon the pureed peaches into four champagne flutes. Top the peach puree with a splash of Crème de framboise and fill with the Italian sparkling wine.

Tip

For a touch of delight, serve these Bellinis with rich shortbread cookies.

FROZEN LEMON DROP
Serves 4

A twist on the popular martini named after a famous hard sugar candy.

4 CUPS CRUSHED ICE CUBES
1 CUP GOOD QUALITY VODKA
1 CUP LEMON SIMPLE SYRUP (RECIPE FOLLOWS)

GARNISH
SUPERFINE SUGAR
4 SLICES LEMON
2 WEDGES OF LEMON

LEMON SIMPLE SYRUP
1 CUP WATER
1 CUP SUGAR
1½ CUPS FRESH LEMON JUICE

Place the ice into the 72 oz. Pitcher, add the vodka and lemon simple syrup and blend on ❸ until smooth.

Garnish: Sprinkle the sugar onto a shallow saucer. Moisten the rim of each martini glass with a lemon wedge, then dip the glass rim into the sugar. Pour the blended Lemon Drop into the prepared martini glasses and serve.

Lemon Simple Syrup: Combine the water and sugar in a small saucepan and bring to a boil. Simmer, while stirring, over low heat until the sugar dissolves. Cool to room temperature, add the lemon juice, and stir until completely combined. Transfer to a glass bottle and store in the refrigerator until use. Makes about 3 cups.

CRÈME DE BANANA
Serves 1

A great way to get your daily servings of fruit!

4 TO 6 CRUSHED ICE CUBES
1 BANANA, PEELED
2 OUNCES LIGHT RUM
2 OUNCES CRÈME DE BANANA
4 OUNCES PINEAPPLE JUICE
SLICE OF FRESH PINEAPPLE FOR GARNISH

Place the ice cubes in the 40 oz. Pitcher and add the remaining ingredients, except the garnish. Blend on ❸ until smooth. Pour into a chilled glass, garnish with the fresh pineapple and serve with a straw.

Tip

To create a spectacular presentation with only two ingredients, shave 4 cups of ice in the *Ninja™ Kitchen System* and divide among 4 glasses. Pour straight shots of Crème de Banana over the ice and serve at once.

HOT APPLE PIE ALA MODE
Serves 2

An apple-licious treat for any season.

2 CUPS VANILLA ICE CREAM
1 CUP CRUSHED ICE CUBES
½ TEASPOON GROUND CINNAMON
½ TEASPOON GROUND NUTMEG
4 OUNCES VANILLA VODKA
4 OUNCES CALVADOS

GARNISH
¼ CUP SUPERFINE SUGAR
⅓ TEASPOON GROUND CINNAMON
WHIPPED CREAM

Place all ingredients, except the garnishes, into the 72 oz. Pitcher and blend on ❸ until smooth. Combine the superfine sugar and cinnamon in a shallow saucer. Moisten the rims of two rocks glasses with calvados and dip the rim in the sugar-cinnamon mixture. Divide the drink between the glasses and top with whipped cream and a sprinkle of cinnamon-sugar.

✳ Tip

Calvados is an apple brandy from Normandy, France, and is well-known for the distinctively rich and smooth apple flavor it imbues into food and drinks. It is well worth the investment to buy Calvados even if you are only going to use it sparingly along the rim of your cocktail glass.

CRUSHED PEPPERMINT SNOWFALL MARTINI

Makes 2 servings

A festive drink, especially around the winter holidays.

1 CUP PEPPERMINT CANDY, UNWRAPPED
2 OUNCES GOOD QUALITY VODKA
1½ OUNCES PEPPERMINT SCHNAPPS
1 OUNCE WHITE CHOCOLATE LIQUEUR
1 OUNCE WHITE CRÈME DE MINT
2 OUNCES HEAVY CREAM

Place the peppermint candy into the 72 oz. Pitcher and blend on ❸ until finely crushed. Pour onto a shallow saucer and set aside. Clean and dry the blender.

Place all the remaining ingredients in the 72 oz. Pitcher and blend on ❶ until smooth. Moisten the rim of each martini glass with Peppermint Schnapps and dip each in crushed peppermint. Fill the prepared glasses with the blended martini.

Tip

Double or triple this recipe for a party. It is a beautiful drink to serve and a minty shot of liqueur on the tongue!

JAMAICAN SCREWDRIVER
Makes 4 servings

The added kick of rum turns this Screwdriver into a "Jamaican-style" pleasure!

6 OUNCES GOOD QUALITY VODKA

4 OUNCES LIGHT RUM

2 CUPS ORANGE JUICE

1 CUP PINEAPPLE JUICE

4 CUPS CRUSHED ICE CUBES

4 ORANGE SLICES FOR GARNISH

Place all the ingredients, except the orange slices, into the 72 oz. Pitcher and blend on ③ until smooth and frothy. Pour into tall chilled glasses and garnish with the orange slices.

Tip

A traditional screwdriver cocktail is simply vodka and orange juice poured over ice, and has been hugely popular for several decades. This variation adds pineapple juice and light rum for more flavor and the frozen blend makes it perfect for brunch or breakfast on a weekend morning.

BUSHWACKER

Makes 2 servings

Beware the Bushwacker! This cocktail really packs a punch, hence the name.

2 OUNCES DARK RUM
2 OUNCES KAHLUA
2 OUNCES DARK CRÈME DE CACAO
2 OUNCES COCONUT LIQUEUR
4 OUNCES HEAVY CREAM
2 CUPS CRUSHED ICE CUBES

GARNISH
WHIPPED CREAM
GROUND NUTMEG

Place all ingredients, except the whipped cream and nutmeg, into the 72 oz. Pitcher and blend on ③ until smooth. Pour into tall glasses and garnish with whipped cream and a sprinkle of nutmeg.

Tip

Change this up by substituting cream of coconut for the coconut liqueur, amaretto for the Kahlua, or try using equal portions of dark and light rum. Every substitution creates an entirely new drink, worthy of tasting and testing among friends!

SOUTH PACIFIC SLUSH

Makes 2 servings

You will be able to hear the ocean breeze blowing through the palm trees as you sip this delicious island sensation.

2 CUPS CRUSHED ICE CUBES
4 OUNCES DARK RUM
4 OUNCES ORANGE JUICE
2 OUNCES COCONUT MILK
1 BANANA, PEELED
2 TABLESPOONS LIME JUICE

GARNISH
8 PINEAPPLE CHUNKS
4 ORANGE WEDGES, HALVED
2 THIN WOODEN SKEWERS
2 SPLASHES GRENADINE

Place the ice cubes in the 72 oz. Pitcher, add the remaining ingredients, except the garnish, and blend on ③ until slushy-smooth.

Thread the pineapple chunks and orange wedges alternately onto skewers. Pour the drinks into tall, chilled glasses and garnish with the fruit skewers and a splash of grenadine.

FRESH PAPAYA
MOJITO FREEZE
P. 83

CHAPTER FOUR

SINGLE SERVE ON-THE-GO RECIPES

BLUEBERRY BLAST
Serves 1

Great for supporting good eyesight, blueberries pack significant amounts of antioxidants in every serving.

½ CUP WHITE GRAPE JUICE
½ CUP LOW FAT PLAIN YOGURT
½ BANANA, PEELED
½ CUP FRESH OR FROZEN WILD BLUEBERRIES, RINSED
8 ICE CUBES

Place all ingredients in the Single Serve Cup and press the Single Serve button until smooth.

POMEGRANATE POWER SMOOTHIE

Serves 1

Boost your mental and immune systems with pomegranate juice.

½ CUP LOW FAT PLAIN YOGURT
½ CUP POMEGRANATE JUICE
½ CUP FROZEN BLUEBERRIES
1 TBSP. RAW, UNFILTERED HONEY

Place all ingredients in the Single Serve Cup and press the Single Serve button until smooth.

CHERRY SMOOTHIE

Serves 1

Like a cherry-chip milkshake!

½ CUP LOW FAT MILK
½ CUP LOW FAT VANILLA YOGURT
½ CUP FRESH SWEET CHERRIES, PITTED (OR USE
FROZEN CHERRIES, IF DESIRED)
½ BANANA, PEELED
5 TO 6 ICE CUBES

Place all ingredients in the Single Serve Cup and press the Single Serve button until smooth.

PEANUT BUTTER CHOCOLATE

Serves 1

Dark chocolate offers surprising health benefits.

¼ CUP LOW FAT MILK
2 TBSP. CREAMY PEANUT BUTTER
¾ CUP LOW FAT VANILLA FROZEN YOGURT
1 OZ. DARK CHOCOLATE

Place all ingredients in the Single Serve Cup and press the Single Serve button until smooth.

VITAMIN C CUCUMBER BLAST

Serves 1

A super good-for-you fruit and vegetable combination!

1 GRAPEFRUIT, PEELED AND QUARTERED
1 ORANGE, PEELED AND QUARTERED
¼ CUCUMBER, PEELED
2-3 ICE CUBES

Place all ingredients in the Single Serve Cup. Press the Single Serve button until smooth.

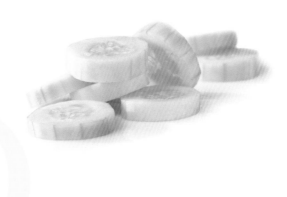

SUMMER BERRY SENSATION

Serves 1

Kick it up by adding any fruit-flavored yogurt!

½ CUP APPLE JUICE
½ CUP LOW FAT VANILLA FROZEN YOGURT
¼ CUP FROZEN RASPBERRIES
¼ CUP FROZEN BLUEBERRIES
¼ CUP FROZEN STRAWBERRIES

Place all ingredients in the Single Serve Cup and press the Single Serve button until smooth.

WATERMELON & LIME SMOOTHIE
Serves 1

Superior anti-aging properties in this light beverage!

¼ CUP WHITE GRAPE JUICE
1 CUP SEEDLESS WATERMELON CHUNKS, FROZEN
½ TSP. LIME ZEST (OPTIONAL)
1 TSP. RAW, UNFILTERED HONEY (OPTIONAL)

Place all ingredients in the Single Serve Cup and press the Single Serve button until smooth.

STRAWBERRY FIELDS

Serves 1

Make this thick and rich strawberry delight your go-to smoothie any morning of the week.

½ CUP ICE CUBES
½ CUP FRESH STRAWBERRIES, HULLED
½ MEDIUM BANANA, PEELED
6 OZ. STRAWBERRY YOGURT
2 TABLESPOONS LOW FAT MILK OR SOY MILK

Place all of the ingredients in the Single Serve Cup and press the Single Serve button until smooth.

ENERGY BINGE

Serves 1

Use any combination of berries you like to create seasonal energy drinks.

½ **CUP ICE CUBES**
¼ **CUP BLACKBERRIES**
¼ **CUP BLUEBERRIES**
¼ **CUP RASPBERRIES**
½ **CUP RASPBERRY YOGURT**
½ **CUP CRANBERRY JUICE**

Place all ingredients in the Single Serve Cup and press the Single Serve button until smooth.

MANGO MENTAL BOOST

Serves 1

Mangos contain lots of potassium and great vitamins – indulge!

½ CUP FROZEN PEACHES, CUT IN CHUNKS
½ CUP FROZEN MANGOS, CUT IN CHUNKS
¾ CUP GREEN TEA, CHILLED
1 TEASPOON HONEY

Place all ingredients in the Single Serve Cup and press the Single Serve button until smooth.

TOMATO SPIKE

Serves 1

This tomato juice is guaranteed to start you day with a kick of energy!

2-3 ICE CUBES
1 MEDIUM TOMATO, SEEDED, CUT IN HALF
½ CUP LOW-SODIUM TOMATO JUICE
2 RADISHES, STEMS REMOVED
¼ JALAPEÑO PEPPER, SEEDED

Place the ingredients in the Single Serve Cup and press the Single Serve button until smooth.

RASPBERRY & GREEN TEA SURGE

Serves 1

Green tea is a superhero in the antioxidant world. It builds your immune system and fights cancer cells.

Place all ingredients in the Single Serve Cup and press the Single Serve button until smooth.

2 ICE CUBES
¾ CUP FRESH RASPBERRIES (OR USE STRAWBERRIES)
½ CUP SWEETENED GREEN TEA, COOLED
½ CUCUMBER, PEELED, CUT IN THIRDS
1 TABLESPOON MINT LEAVES

SHOT OF SUPER C

Serves 1

Packing almost 200 milligrams of vitamin C, this shot is the perfect way to build your immunity.

½ **CUP ICE CUBES**
½ **SMALL NAVAL ORANGE, PEELED (OR USE TANGELOS OR MINNEOLAS)**
½ **SMALL GRAPEFRUIT, PEELED**
½ **CUP PINEAPPLE JUICE**

Place all ingredients in the Single Serve Cup and press the Single Serve button until smooth.

BLACKBERRY LIGHT
Serves 1

Blackberries are an easy way to maintain your weight because they are full of fiber, vitamins and minerals.

½ **CUP ICE CUBES**
½ **CUP BLACKBERRIES**
½ **CUP NONFAT LEMON YOGURT**
½ **RIPE PAPAYA, SEEDED, CUT IN CHUNKS**
¼ **CUP LOWFAT MILK**

Place all the ingredients in the Single Serve Cup and press the Single Serve button until smooth.

MANGO BANANA SLIDE

Serves 1

This quick-to-prepare juice helps keep your metabolism balanced!

½ CUP ICE CUBES
½ MANGO, PITTED, PEELED, CUT IN QUARTERS
½ MEDIUM RIPE BANANA, PEELED, CUT IN HALF
1 MANDARIN ORANGE, PEELED, SEGMENTED

Place all ingredients in the Single Serve Cup and press the Single Serve button until smooth.

FRESH PAPAYA MOJITO FREEZE
Serves 1

Spiced rum gives this frozen cocktail a caramelized sugar kick!

½ CUP ICE CUBES
2 OZ. SPICED RUM (SUCH AS CAPTAIN MORGAN'S®)
¼ RIPE PAPAYA, PEELED, SEEDED, CUT IN CHUNKS
2 OZ. CLUB SODA
1 TEASPOON LIME JUICE
1 TEASPOON SUGAR, OPTIONAL
4 MINT LEAVES

Place all the ingredients in the Single Serve Cup and press the Single Serve button until smooth.

MINI CRAB CAKES
WITH DILL SAUCE
P. 91

CHAPTER FIVE

APPETIZERS, DIPS & SPREADS

WARM DIJON CHICKEN SPREAD

Serves 6 to 8

Savory and filling, with tangy Dijon mustard throughout.

1 TABLESPOON SOFT BUTTER

3 LARGE SLICES YELLOW ONION, SEPARATED INTO RINGS

½ CUP MAYONNAISE (REGULAR OR LOWFAT)

¼ CUP MILK

1 TABLESPOON FRESH ITALIAN PARSLEY, MINCED, PLUS MORE FOR GARNISH

½ TEASPOON SALT

¼ TEASPOON PEPPER

3 TABLESPOONS DIJON MUSTARD

2 CUPS COOKED CHICKEN, BONELESS AND SKINLESS

1 LOAF FRENCH OR THIN SOURDOUGH BREAD, SLICED THINLY AND TOASTED

In a sauté pan, melt the butter over medium heat. Add the onion rings and sauté for 6 to 8 minutes, or until lightly caramelized. Remove from the heat and cool slightly.

Place the mayonnaise, milk, parsley, salt, pepper, mustard, and chicken in the 72 oz. Pitcher and add the cooked onion. Blend on ❶ for 30 seconds, or until uniformly mixed. Use a spatula to clean the sides of the pitcher and blend again, if needed. Add a few drops of milk, if needed. Taste and adjust the seasonings to your liking. In a glass serving dish, briefly heat the chicken spread in the microwave oven for 30 seconds to 1 minute to warm the spread thoroughly. Garnish the spread with parsley and serve on the pieces of toasted bread.

OLIVE TAPENADE BRUSCHETTA

Serves 8

Toss together green and black olives with capers for an intriguing twist on bruschetta.

6 OUNCE CAN BLACK OLIVES, DRAINED
4 OUNCE CAN GREEN OLIVES, DRAINED
3 TABLESPOONS CAPERS, RINSED
1 CLOVE GARLIC, PEELED
1 TABLESPOON LEMON JUICE
2 TABLESPOONS EXTRA-VIRGIN OLIVE OIL
1 BAGUETTE FRENCH BREAD, SLICED AND TOASTED

Place the black and green olives in the 72 oz. Pitcher and add the capers, garlic, lemon juice, and olive oil. Blend on ❶ until uniform, but not completely smooth. To serve, spread the olive tapenade on toasted slices of French bread.

Tip

Tapenade is equally at home served on bread or mixed with tomatoes and served over pita chips as a Mediterranean salsa of sorts. The sharp piquant flavors accent almost any bread or cracker flavor.

CREAM CHEESE FRUIT DIP
WITH STRAWBERRIES

Makes about 2 cups of fruit dip

A summery appetizer or a dessert?
You'll have to make this delicious decision.

2 TABLESPOONS ORANGE JUICE
8 OUNCES CREAM CHEESE (WHIPPED
OR REGULAR)
7 OUNCE JAR MARSHMALLOW CRÈME
1 TEASPOON LEMON ZEST, GRATED
3 CUPS FRESH, RIPE STRAWBERRIES,
HULLED AND CLEANED

Pour the juice into the 72 oz. Pitcher and add the cream cheese, marshmallow crème and lemon zest. Blend on **3** until smooth, about 20 seconds. Use a spatula to clean the sides of the pitcher and blend again, if needed.

Spoon the fruit dip into a serving dish and serve with the strawberries on the side.

✳ Tip

Because this dip is sweet, yet cream cheese tangy, partner it with slices of pound cake or spread it on cinnamon toast for a new twist. After one taste, you'll find a million delicious variations of your own.

HOT ARTICHOKE DIP
WITH SOURDOUGH ROUNDS

Serves 8

A warm, melty artichoke dip that practically begs for soft sourdough bread. Enjoy with a glass of chilled chardonnay.

1 CUP REDUCED-FAT MAYONNAISE

4 OUNCE CAN MARINATED ARTICHOKES, RESERVE 2 TABLESPOONS LIQUID

½ POUND LOWFAT MOZZARELLA CHEESE, CUT INTO LARGE PIECES

½ CUP PARMESAN CHEESE, CUT INTO PIECES OR GRATED

2 GREEN ONIONS, SLICED

1 ROUND SOURDOUGH BREAD, CUT INTO 2-INCH PIECES

Preheat the oven to 350°F. Place the mayonnaise, artichokes with 2 tablespoons liquid, mozzarella cheese and Parmesan cheese in the 72 oz. Pitcher. Blend on ❷ for 20 seconds. Use a spatula to clean the sides of the pitcher and blend again on ❷ until uniformly smooth. Spoon the dip into a heat-proof serving dish.

Bake the artichoke dip for 20 minutes or until heated through completely. Serve the dip with a wide knife for spreading on the sourdough bread.

✳ Tip

If you like to prep in advance, place the prepared dip in a small slow cooker and cook on low heat for 4 hours. Stir just before serving.

MINI CRAB CAKES WITH DILL SAUCE
Serves 4

A smooth dill sauce accompanies each mini crab cake.

DILL SAUCE
1 CUP FAT-REDUCED MAYONNAISE
2 TABLESPOONS CREAM OR MILK
2 TABLESPOONS FRESH DILL, CHOPPED
2 TABLESPOONS WHITE ONION, ROUGHLY CUT
1 TEASPOON LEMON JUICE
½ TEASPOON SALT

MINI CRAB CAKES
1 POUND FRESH CRABMEAT, PICKED THROUGH & CLEANED
1 LARGE EGG, BEATEN
1 CUP CRUSHED SALTINE CRACKER CRUMBS
3 TABLESPOONS PARMESAN CHEESE
1 SPRIG FRESH PARSLEY
1 CLOVE GARLIC, PEELED
¼ SMALL ONION, PEELED
½ TEASPOON SALT
VEGETABLE OIL FOR FRYING
PARSLEY FOR GARNISH

Dill Sauce: Place all of the ingredients in the 72 oz. Pitcher. Blend on ❸ until uniform. Remove and spoon into a small serving dish. Refrigerate until use.

Mini Crab Cakes: Place the crabmeat, egg, cracker crumbs, cheese, parsley, garlic, onion and salt in the 72 oz. Pitcher. Blend on ❶ for 10 seconds. Use a spatula to clean the sides of the pitcher and blend again on ❶ until almost smooth.

Shape the crabmeat mixture into small, walnut-sized balls. Flatten slightly to form a small cake shape. In a large skillet, add enough vegetable oil to cover about ½-inch of the depth of the pan. Heat the oil to 350°F.

Carefully place the mini crab cakes in the oil to form a single layer. Fry for 1 minute; turn and fry for 1 to 2 minutes, or until cooked through. Remove from the oil with a slotted spoon and drain briefly on paper towels. Repeat with the remaining cakes.

Serve the cakes while hot with a small spoonful of the dill sauce on top of each. Add a small piece of parsley to finish the appetizer.

CHILI CON QUESO WITH TEX MEX SALSA
Serves 6 to 8

Yummy cheese dip with fresh salsa!

2 TABLESPOONS BUTTER
2 TABLESPOONS FLOUR
1 CUP MILK
4 CUPS CHEDDAR CHEESE, GRATED
½ TEASPOON SALT
1 SMALL YELLOW ONION, QUARTERED
½ GREEN PEPPER, SEEDED
3 CLOVES GARLIC, PEELED
1 JALAPEÑO PEPPER, SEEDED

TEX MEX SALSA
2 RIPE TOMATOES, QUARTERED
¼ SMALL ONION
½ JALAPEÑO PEPPER, SEEDED
1 SPRIG FRESH CILANTRO
SALT AND PEPPER TO TASTE
TORTILLA CHIPS

In a saucepan, heat the butter on medium heat. Stir and add the flour, cooking until smooth. Slowly add the milk as the mixture thickens. Add the cheese and stir well. Add salt to taste. Remove from the heat and cool slightly.

Place the yellow onion, green pepper, garlic and jalapeño pepper in the 72 oz. Pitcher. Blend on on ❶ just until chopped. Add the cheese sauce through the lid pour tab and blend again briefly on ❶. Pour into a serving dish and set aside.

To make the Tex Mex Salsa, place the tomatoes, onion, pepper, cilantro, salt and pepper in the 72 oz. Pitcher and blend on ❶ just until chunky. To serve, spoon the queso over the chips and garnish with the salsa.

BLUE CHEESE SLIDERS

Serves 6 to 12 as appetizers or 4 as a main course

A hearty appetizer or casual entrée, these sliders marry grilled onions and a bold blue cheese spread for added oomph.

BLUE CHEESE SPREAD

1 CUP SOUR CREAM (REGULAR OR LOWFAT)
1 CUP MAYONNAISE (REGULAR OR LOWFAT)
4 OUNCES BLUE CHEESE, CRUMBLED
1 CLOVE GARLIC, PEELED
2 GREEN ONIONS, CHOPPED
PINCH SALT

SLIDERS

1½ POUNDS LEAN GROUND BEEF
½ TEASPOON SALT
½ TEASPOON GARLIC SALT
½ TEASPOON BLACK PEPPER
12 SMALL ROLLS OR BUNS, SPLIT HORIZONTALLY, TOASTED
12 SMALL PIECES OF LETTUCE
12 THIN SLICES ROMA TOMATOES

Blue Cheese Spread: Combine all ingredients in the 40 oz. Pitcher. Blend on ③ until smooth. Spoon into a bowl and refrigerate until use.

Sliders: In a large bowl, lightly toss together the beef, salt, garlic salt, and pepper. Form into small patties about the 1½ inches in diameter to form a total of 12 patties. Broil or grill each to your preference.

To assemble the sliders, place a small amount of the blue cheese spread on both sides of one roll. Top with a small piece of lettuce, a beef patty and a tomato slice. Cover with the remaining half roll.

WHITE BEAN & SAGE SPREAD

Serves 6

A simple spread with a hearty, savory impact!

**14 OUNCE CAN CANNELLONI BEANS,
DRAINED, 3 TABLESPOONS LIQUID RESERVED
¼ CUP EXTRA-VIRGIN OLIVE OIL
1 TABLESPOON FRESH SAGE LEAVES
½ TEASPOON SALT
¼ TEASPOON WHITE PEPPER
¼ CUP PARMESAN CHEESE, GRATED
PITA BREAD, TORN INTO SMALL PIECES**

Preheat the oven to 350°F. Place the beans and reserved liquid in the 72 oz. Pitcher. Add the oil, sage leaves, salt, and pepper. Blend on ❷ for 20 seconds. Use a spatula to clean the sides of the pitcher and blend again on ❷ until mostly smooth throughout. Spoon the dip into a heatproof serving dish and cover with the Parmesan cheese.

Bake the spread for 20 minutes, or until piping hot. Offer the spread with the pita bread pieces.

✳ Tip

Although this tastes very rich and smooth, your guests will be surprised to learn that the ingredients are a good-for-you combination of protein-rich beans, olive oil and cheese. Serve with whole wheat crackers or any other sturdy cracker or bread.

GRILLED SHRIMP WITH FRESH PEACH SALSA
Serves 4

Grilled shrimp has a slightly sweet and mild flavor, perfectly accentuated by the tangy, spicy peach salsa.

FRESH PEACH SALSA

2 FRESH, RIPE PEACHES, PITTED AND PEELED
½ FRESH MANGO, PEELED
¼ FRESH PINEAPPLE, PEELED
2 SPRIGS FRESH CILANTRO
¼ SMALL WHITE ONION, PEELED

GRILLED SHRIMP

1 TABLESPOON LEMON JUICE
1 CLOVE GARLIC, MINCED
2 TABLESPOONS SOY SAUCE
¼ CUP VEGETABLE OIL
1 POUND FRESH SHRIMP, PEELED, TAILS REMOVED
CILANTRO FOR GARNISH

Fresh Peach Salsa: Place all ingredients into the 72 oz. Pitcher and pulse on ❶ until chunky, about 15 seconds. Remove and refrigerate until ready to use.

Grilled Shrimp: Place the lemon juice, garlic, soy sauce and oil in a plastic self-sealing bag. Add the shrimp and refrigerate for 1 hour. Thread the shrimp onto wooden or metal skewers and grill over medium heat for 2 minutes on each side, or until cooked through. Shrimp are done when they turn opaque and pink.

Serve the shrimp skewers on small plates accompanied by the salsa. Garnish with additional cilantro if desired.

CHICKEN
TORTILLA SOUP
P. 103

CHAPTER SIX

SOUPS, BISQUE & SAUCES

GAZPACHO

Makes 4 to 6 servings

This age-old soup from Spain originally took hours to make using a mortar and pestle. With the *Ninja™ Kitchen System*, your soup is finished in just a few minutes! For a traditional version that includes day-old French bread, soak the bread in water and squeeze out the excess. Blend with the vegetables to create a heavier soup.

1 LARGE CUCUMBER, PEELED AND
CUT INTO PIECES
1 RED BELL PEPPER, CORED, SEEDED,
AND QUARTERED
1 GREEN BELL PEPPER, CORED, SEEDED,
AND QUARTERED
4 RIPE TOMATOES, CORED AND QUARTERED
1 RED ONION, PEELED AND QUARTERED
4 CLOVES GARLIC, PEELED
½ BUNCH FLAT LEAF PARSLEY, STEMMED
1½ CUPS TOMATO JUICE
2 TABLESPOONS RED WINE VINEGAR
2 TABLESPOONS OLIVE OIL, (OPTIONAL)
2 TEASPOONS GROUND PAPRIKA
½ TEASPOON SALT
½ TEASPOON FRESHLY GROUND BLACK PEPPER

Place the cucumber, bell peppers, tomatoes, onion, garlic and parsley into the 72 oz. Pitcher and pulse until the vegetables are coarsely chopped. Transfer half of the vegetable mixture into a large mixing bowl. Add the remaining ingredients to the pitcher and blend on ❷ until smooth. Add the smooth vegetable mixture to the mixing bowl, stirring well to incorporate all ingredients.

Cover tightly and refrigerate for at least 2 hours or until well-chilled. The longer the soup sits, the more flavor it develops. Taste and adjust seasonings as desired. Serve in chilled bowls with sliced cucumber, bell peppers, and chopped parsley as fresh summer croutons.

CREAMY AVOCADO SOUP

Makes 4 to 6 servings

With all the flavors of guacamole, this soup is the perfect starter for a festive Mexican dinner.

2 LARGE RIPE AVOCADOS, PEELED, PITTED AND QUARTERED
8 GREEN ONIONS, CLEANED
2 CUPS CHICKEN STOCK, WARMED (VEGETABLE STOCK MAY BE USED IF DESIRED)
2 TABLESPOONS FRESH LIME JUICE
2 TABLESPOONS FRESH CILANTRO, CHOPPED
½ TEASPOON SALT
¾ TEASPOON CUMIN OR MORE TO TASTE
½ TEASPOON RED CHILE POWDER OR MORE TO TASTE
1 CUP HEAVY CREAM
4 TO 6 SPRIGS CILANTRO FOR GARNISH

Place the avocado, green onions, chicken stock, lime juice, chopped cilantro, salt, cumin, and red chile powder into the 72 oz. Pitcher and blend on ② until just mixed. Add the heavy cream and blend again until the soup is just smooth. Do not over-blend. Taste and adjust the seasonings as desired.

Serve at room temperature or cover and refrigerate for at least 2 hours to serve chilled. Garnish with a sprig of cilantro before serving.

SUMMER STRAWBERRY MINT SOUP
Makes 4 servings

Pack this chilled soup in a thermos for a special addition to any picnic.

2 CUPS WATER
4 CUPS FRESH STRAWBERRIES, STEMMED AND HULLED (OR USE FROZEN, THAWED STRAWBERRIES)
2 TABLESPOONS SUPERFINE WHITE SUGAR
1 TABLESPOON FRESH LIME JUICE
½ CUP GOOD QUALITY CHARDONNAY
6 LARGE MINT LEAVES, CHOPPED (ABOUT 4 TABLESPOONS)

GARNISH
4 SPRIGS OF MINT FOR GARNISH
½ CUP GREEK YOGURT FOR GARNISH

Place all ingredients, except the garnishes, into the 72 oz. Pitcher and blend on ❶ until smooth. Cover and refrigerate for 2 hours to chill. (If you prefer, serve at room temperature.) Serve in bowls with a dollop of yogurt and garnish with a mint sprig.

Tip
You can't imagine how wonderful this chilled soup is on a hot summer day! Add a meal of cooked cold shrimp or crab over greens dressed with a light vinaigrette and you have a meal fit for royalty.

CHICKEN TORTILLA SOUP

Makes 4 to 6 servings

A yummy soup with rich flavor and texture!

1 LARGE WHITE ONION, PEELED AND QUARTERED

3 CLOVES GARLIC, PEELED

4 JALAPEÑO PEPPERS, SEEDED

1 RED BELL PEPPER, CORED AND SEEDED

2 TEASPOONS EXTRA-VIRGIN OLIVE OIL

8 OUNCE CAN CRUSHED TOMATOES

3 TABLESPOONS FRESH CILANTRO, CHOPPED

(1 TABLESPOON IS RESERVED FOR GARNISH)

4 TO 6 CUPS CHICKEN STOCK

2 TABLESPOONS FRESH LIME JUICE

1 TEASPOON GROUND CUMIN

½ TEASPOON SALT (OR TO TASTE)

1 TEASPOON FRESHLY GROUND BLACK PEPPER

4 6-INCH CORN TORTILLAS

2 CUPS CHICKEN, COOKED AND SHREDDED

1 AVOCADO, PITTED, PEELED, AND DICED

1 CUP JACK CHEESE, SHREDDED

2 CUPS TORTILLA CHIPS, CRUMBLED

1 LIME, CUT INTO WEDGES

Place the onion, garlic, peppers and red pepper in the 72 oz. Pitcher and pulse on ① until chopped. Heat the oil in a stockpot over medium heat. Add the chopped vegetables, tomatoes, and 2 tablespoons of cilantro. Sauté and stir for about 5 minutes, or until the vegetables soften. Add the chicken stock, juice, cumin, salt and pepper. Reduce the heat and simmer until the vegetables are tender, about 15 minutes.

Place two-thirds of the soup into the pitcher. Briefly heat the corn tortillas in a dry skillet over medium heat just until softened. Tear the tortillas into pieces, add to the pitcher and blend on ② until the mixture is fairly smooth and thick. Pour the blended soup back into the stockpot, stirring well to incorporate.

Divide the shredded chicken between 4 soup bowls. Ladle the hot soup into the bowls and top with diced avocado, Jack cheese and crumbled tortilla strips. Garnish the soup with the remaining chopped cilantro and lime wedges.

CLASSIC LOBSTER BISQUE
Serves 4

Lobster Bisque is the height of elegance! Use your *Ninja™ Kitchen System* to cut your prep time and eliminate major mistakes.

1 MEDIUM CARROT, PEELED AND ROUGHLY CHOPPED

1 MEDIUM ONION, PEELED AND ROUGHLY CHOPPED

1 INSIDE STALK CELERY, PEELED, STRINGS REMOVED AND ROUGHLY CHOPPED

½ CUP UNSALTED BUTTER, DIVIDED

2 UNCOOKED LOBSTER TAILS, WITH SHELLS

¼ CUP PALE DRY SHERRY OR BRANDY

¼ CUP DRY WHITE WINE

6 CUPS FISH STOCK

1 TABLESPOON TOMATO PASTE

1 BAY LEAF

6 SPRIGS FRESH PARSLEY

2 STEMS FRESH THYME

3 TABLESPOONS WHITE FLOUR

1 CUP HEAVY CREAM

SALT AND WHITE PEPPER TO TASTE

BRANDY AS GARNISH

Place the carrot, onion and celery into the 72 oz. Pitcher and blend on ❷ until the vegetables are minced. In a heavy-bottomed soup pot, melt half the butter over medium-low heat and add the carrots, onion, celery and the lobster tails in shells. Sauté 3 to 4 minutes. Add the sherry, wine, fish stock, tomato paste and herbs and simmer the stock for 30 to 40 minutes. Remove the lobsters from the stock, remove the meat from the shells and cut into large chunks, setting aside. Strain the stock through a sieve.

In a large saucepan over medium heat, melt the remaining butter. Whisk in the flour, stirring to make a roux. Steadily, whisk in the strained lobster stock, until smoothly blended.

Transfer the soup into the pitcher, in batches as needed, and blend on ❷ until smooth. Return the soup to the stockpot, add the lobster and cream and simmer, stirring frequently for 10 minutes. Adjust the seasonings, if desired. To serve, pour the soup into bowls and add a splash of brandy on top. Store any leftovers in the refrigerator.

CREAM OF BROCCOLI SOUP
Serves 6 to 8

This delectable soup uses potatoes to thicken the delicious stock, cutting out much of the usual cream and creating a healthier version of a favorite comfort food.

2 TABLESPOONS BUTTER
1 TABLESPOON EXTRA-VIRGIN OLIVE OIL
1 MEDIUM SHALLOT, PEELED AND CHOPPED
1 LARGE RUSSET POTATO, PEELED AND DICED
1 CUP WATER
1 CUP CHICKEN STOCK
1 MEDIUM HEAD OF BROCCOLI, CUT INTO FLORETS, STOCK PEELED AND CHUNKED
½ TEASPOON SALT
½ TEASPOON WHITE PEPPER
¾ CUP HEAVY CREAM
¼ TEASPOON GROUND NUTMEG

Heat the butter and oil over medium-low heat in a medium saucepan; add the shallot, cover and sweat, stirring occasionally, until softened. Add the diced potato, water and chicken stock. Increase the heat and bring just to a boil. Reduce the heat to medium-low and simmer, stirring occasionally for 8 minutes. Add the broccoli, salt, and pepper and simmer for an additional 5 to 6 minutes, depending on the size of dice, until the potatoes and broccoli are tender.

Allow the soup to cool until just warm, then ladle in batches into the 72 oz. Pitcher. Blend on ❷ until very smooth. Add the cream and nutmeg and pulse to incorporate. Pour the soup back into the saucepan and cook over medium heat to thicken slightly. Taste and adjust the seasonings before serving.

POTATO & CORN CHOWDER
Makes 6 to 8 servings

This "stick to your ribs," hearty soup is sure to become a family favorite. The green chile adds that mildly spicy taste of the Southwest.

4 SLICES APPLE-WOOD SMOKED BACON
1 LARGE ONION, PEELED AND CHOPPED
1 GREEN BELL PEPPER, CORED, SEEDED AND CHOPPED
4 MEDIUM RUSSET POTATOES, PEELED AND DICED
2 CUPS CHICKEN STOCK
½ TEASPOON FRESHLY GROUND BLACK PEPPER
2 CUPS FRESH OR FROZEN CORN KERNELS
2 CUPS WHOLE MILK
4 OUNCE CAN CHOPPED NEW MEXICAN GREEN CHILIES
1 CUP HEAVY CREAM
PINCH SALT (OPTIONAL)
4 TABLESPOONS FRESH CHIVES, MINCED

Cook the bacon in a stockpot over medium-high heat until crisp. Drain on paper towels and crumble when cooled. Pour off all but about 3 tablespoons of the bacon drippings, re-heat and add the onion, green pepper and potatoes. Stir to coat and sauté for 3 to 4 minutes. Add the chicken stock and pepper and reduce the heat to medium-low. Cook, stirring occasionally, for 8 minutes.

While the potatoes are cooking, place 1 cup of corn and 1 cup of milk into the 72 oz. Pitcher and blend on ❷ until roughly uniform. Add the blended mixture to the potatoes, along with the remaining corn, milk and the green chile. Continue cooking until the corn and potatoes are tender.

Stir in the heavy cream and simmer for a few additional minutes. Taste and adjust the seasonings as desired. Serve in soup bowls garnished with the chives and generous amounts of crumbled bacon.

FRESH TOMATO BASIL SOUP

Makes 4 servings

In the summer months, this is a great way to use tomatoes ripening in your garden. Run them through a food mill to remove skin and seeds, but retain all that powerful, antioxidant juice.

1 TEASPOON EXTRA-VIRGIN OLIVE OIL
1 SMALL YELLOW ONION, PEELED AND CHOPPED
1 MEDIUM SHALLOT, PEELED AND CHOPPED
3 MEDIUM TOMATOES, SEEDED AND CHOPPED (OR 28 OUNCE CAN WHOLE TOMATOES)
1½ CUPS VEGETABLE STOCK
1 CUP HEAVY CREAM
½ TEASPOON SALT
½ TEASPOON WHITE PEPPER
1 TEASPOON FRESH THYME LEAVES
½ CUP PACKED FRESH BASIL
6 LARGE FRESH BASIL LEAVES, STACKED, ROLLED LENGTHWISE AND THINLY SLICED (CHIFFONADE), FOR GARNISH

Heat the oil in a large stockpot over medium-low heat. Add the onion and shallots, cover the pan and sweat, stirring occasionally, until softened, but not browned. Add the tomatoes, vegetable stock, cream, salt, pepper, and thyme and simmer for 10 minutes, stirring occasionally. Stir in the ½ cup basil.

Cool the soup until just warm, then transfer the soup in batches to the 72 oz. Pitcher and blend on ❷ until smooth. Return the soup to the stockpot to re-heat over low heat. Do not allow the soup to boil. Taste and adjust the seasonings as desired. Serve in soup bowls with a sprinkling of the chiffonade basil.

VICHYSSOISE
Serves 4 to 6

Leeks are grown in sandy soil and are notoriously difficult to clean. The best way is to slice off one-fourth inch of the root end and cut lengthwise only through the white and light green part, leaving the dark green leaves intact. Turn the leek a quarter turn and repeat, cutting the leek into quarters lengthwise, still leaving the dark green leaves intact. Rinse white and light green section of leek under cool running water, fanning them apart to expose the dirt and sand.

2 LARGE LEEKS, WHITE PART ONLY, CLEANED WELL
2 MEDIUM RUSSET POTATOES, PEELED AND DICED
2 CUPS WATER
2 CUPS CHICKEN STOCK
½ TEASPOON SALT
½ TEASPOON WHITE PEPPER
1 CUP HEAVY CREAM
1 TABLESPOON FRESH CHIVES, MINCED

In a heavy bottomed stockpot, bring the leeks, potatoes, water, chicken stock, salt and pepper to a boil. Partially cover the pan and reduce to a simmer for 20 to 30 minutes, or until the potatoes and leeks are tender.

Stir in the heavy cream and transfer the soup, in batches, to the 72 oz. Pitcher. Blend on ❷ until smooth. Taste and adjust the seasonings as desired. Refrigerate the soup for at least 2 hours to serve chilled, or return the soup to the stockpot and heat over medium-low to serve warm. Garnish with minced chives.

CLASSIC HOLLANDAISE SAUCE

Make about 3/4 cup

Using the *Ninja™ Kitchen System* Pitcher takes care of the problem of separation and turns this sometimes troublesome preparation into the easiest sauce ever. A lovely Hollandaise sauce always adds a touch of sophistication to a vegetable dish or your Sunday eggs. Enjoy!

3 LARGE EGG YOLKS
1 TEASPOON FRESH LEMON JUICE
PINCH DRY MUSTARD
PINCH CAYENNE PEPPER
PINCH SALT
2 CUPS UNSALTED BUTTER
A FEW TABLESPOONS OF HOT WATER TO THIN AS NECESSARY

Place the egg yolks, lemon juice, mustard, cayenne pepper and salt in the 72 oz. Pitcher and blend on ① until combined, cleaning the sides of the blender with a spatula if needed.

In a small sauce pan, melt the butter, skimming the foam off the top. Discard the foam. Gently pour the clarified butter off of the milk solids that have settled in the bottom of the pan. With the blender running on ②, slowly pour the melted butter, in a thin stream, through the top pour tab, into the egg mixture. As the sauce thickens, continue blending until the sauce is smooth and as thin as you prefer. Add water as necessary, a tablespoon at a time, to prevent the Hollandaise Sauce from over-thickening. Serve at once or keep warm over a pan of hot water.

BASIL PESTO
Makes about 2 cups

A versatile sauce to have on hand in the fridge or freezer. Toss with pasta, use as a marinade or a sauce for fish or chicken. Substitute spinach, roasted red pepper or broccoli for a twist on this classic.

½ CUP TOASTED PINE NUTS
2 LARGE CLOVES GARLIC, PEELED
4 CUPS TIGHTLY PACKED FRESH BASIL LEAVES
½ CUP FRESHLY GRATED PARMESAN CHEESE
½ TEASPOON SALT
½ TEASPOON FRESHLY GROUND BLACK PEPPER
½ TO ¾ CUP EXTRA VIRGIN OLIVE OIL

Place all of the ingredients, except the olive oil, into the 72 oz. Pitcher and blend on ❷ until combined, but still containing some texture.

With the unit running on ❷, drizzle the olive oil through the top pour tab and blend until smooth. Use right away or store in the refrigerator for up to 4 days until use.

Tip

It's ridiculously easy to make pesto and it's also tremendously easy to grow your own basil. Try planting a small herb garden and make basil your centerpiece. Basil will grow in full sun with a little bit of water and loving care – not much else is needed for success. Vacuum bag and freeze the basil pesto in small portions for quick and easy use all year long.

HOMEMADE PIZZA SAUCE

Makes about 1 3/4 cups, or enough for 2 pizzas

Fresh pizza dough is so easy – check it out on page XX. All you need to add is this delightfully fresh sauce. Use this along with your favorite toppings for the perfect addition to a fun family movie night.

6 OUNCE CAN TOMATO PASTE
1 CUP WARM WATER
2 CLOVES GARLIC, PEELED
6 LARGE LEAVES FRESH BASIL
½ TEASPOON ONION POWDER
¼ TEASPOON DRIED OREGANO
¼ TEASPOON DRIED MARJORAM
½ TEASPOON FRESHLY GROUND BLACK PEPPER
½ TEASPOON SALT
½ TEASPOON DRIED RED PEPPER FLAKES

Place all of the ingredients in the 40 oz. Pitcher and blend on ❷ until thoroughly combined. Adjust the seasonings to your taste and add a pinch of sugar if you want to balance the acidity of the tomatoes.

Tip

Make a double-batch of this sauce and freeze half for another night. Pair it with hot pasta and a grating of fresh Parmesan, pour it over chicken breasts and bake with mozzarella cheese, the list of uses is endless!

SOUTH AMERICAN CHIMICHURRI SAUCE

Makes 1 to 1 1/2 cups

There are many versions of this classic South American accompaniment for grilled meats. This recipe is a good, solid place to start using your imagination, as you add ingredients to your taste.

1 BUNCH FRESH PARSLEY, CLEANED, LARGE STEMS REMOVED
10 LARGE CLOVES GARLIC, PEELED
1 TEASPOON SALT
1 CUP EXTRA-VIRGIN OLIVE OIL

OPTIONAL INGREDIENTS

1 SMALL WHITE ONION, PEELED AND QUARTERED
½ CUP WHITE WINE VINEGAR
½ TEASPOON FRESH GROUND PEPPER
1 TEASPOON FRESH BASIL, THYME OR OREGANO OR A MIXTURE OF ANY FAVORITE HERBS

Place the parsley, garlic, salt and oil (and optional ingredients) into the 40 oz. Pitcher and blend on ① until finely chopped. Serve right away or store in a covered glass dish in the refrigerator for several days.

Tip

Chimichurri Sauce is more like a pesto with a hefty garlic flavor than it is a sauce and it has become increasing popular all over the world. Try it on tender lamb chops, beef kebabs, or any simple cut of beef, pork, or chicken.

CHIPOTLE TARTAR SAUCE
Makes 1 1/2 cups

Try this tangy twist on the traditional Tartar Sauce. Especially tasty with crunchy fried calamari or onion rings.

1 CUP REGULAR OR LOWFAT MAYONNAISE
2 SMALL CHIPOTLE PEPPERS
¼ CUP SWEET PICKLE, DICED
1 TEASPOON JUICE FROM CANNED CHIPOTLES
2 TEASPOONS WHOLE GRAIN MUSTARD
2 TABLESPOON WHITE WINE VINEGAR
1 TEASPOON FRESHLY GROUND BLACK PEPPER
½ TEASPOON SALT

Place all of the ingredients into the 72 oz. Pitcher and pulse on ❶ until the pickles are finely chopped and the tartar sauce is well blended, but not pureed. Transfer to a serving bowl or cover and store in the refrigerator.

Tip

A Chipotle pepper is a ripe, smoked jalapeño pepper that offers rich, smoked and very spicy flavors. A little goes a long way, particularly when you also use the adobo sauce packed with chipotles in cans.

PEANUT DIPPING SAUCE

Makes 1 1/2 cups

This sauce is a snap to prepare and can be used with just about any vegetable or chicken dish as a way to enliven your meal. If your kids like peanut butter, they will eat just about anything dipped in this sauce.

½ CUP HOT WATER
½ CUP CRUNCHY PEANUT BUTTER
⅓ CUP HOISEN SAUCE (OR SUBSTITUTE SOY SAUCE)
1 TABLESPOON ASIAN RED CHILI PASTE
1 TABLESPOON FRESH LIME JUICE

Place all of the ingredients into the 40 oz. Pitcher and blend on ❷ until completely combined. Taste and the adjust flavors and consistency to your liking.

Tip

This sauce also makes a delicious base for chicken lettuce wraps. Mince cooked chicken on ❶, add 3 to 4 tablespoons of this sauce, and wrap in crisp lettuce leaves for a wonderful appetizer or snack.

PECAN
CINNAMON
ROLLS
P. 126

CHAPTER SEVEN

BREADS & BAKERY GOODS

EASY PIZZA DOUGH

Makes 1 pizza crust

So incredibly easy when you make it in your *Ninja™ Kitchen System!* Start with this basic dough to make pizza crust, foccacia bread, calzones, rolls and bread sticks.

¼ OUNCE PKG. DRY ACTIVE YEAST
1 TEASPOON SALT
1 TABLESPOON SUGAR
⅔ CUP WATER, WARMED TO 110-115°F
¼ CUP CANOLA OIL (SUBSTITUTE OLIVE OIL)
2 CUPS ALL-PURPOSE FLOUR

Position the Dough Station as directed and insert the Dough Hook into the 40 oz. Pitcher. Place the yeast, salt, sugar and water in the pitcher. Blend on ① for 10 seconds. Add the oil and flour, 1 cup at a time, pulsing on ① until the dough is smooth and no lumps remain. Transfer the dough to a lightly-oiled bowl and cover. Let rise for about 1 hour.

If you are making high-rise pizza dough, punch down the dough and let rise again for 45 minutes. If not, eliminate the second rising and spread the dough onto a pizza pan or baking sheet that has been lightly coated with cooking spray.

Add sauce and toppings as preferred and bake at 425°F for 25-30 minutes, or until the crust is lightly browned and the toppings and cheese are hot.

BUTTERMILK BREAD

Makes 1 golden loaf

Offering a yeasty, homemade aroma and melt-in-your-mouth flavor, this bread doesn't disappoint!

¼ OZ. PKG DRY ACTIVE YEAST
¼ CUP WATER, WARMED TO 110-115°F
2 TABLESPOONS SUGAR
½ CUP LOWFAT BUTTERMILK
1 TEASPOON SALT
¼ CUP VEGETABLE OIL
1 LARGE EGG, BEATEN
3¼ CUPS ALL-PURPOSE FLOUR

Place the yeast and warm water in a small bowl and stir well until the yeast is dissolved. Add the sugar and stir again. Let stand for about 5 minutes.

Position the Dough Station as directed and insert the Dough Hook into the 40 oz. Pitcher. Place the buttermilk, salt, oil, egg and yeast mixture in the pitcher and blend on ① for about 20 seconds. Add 1 cup of flour and blend on ① until the flour is incorporated. Use a spatula to clean the sides of the pitcher. Add 1 cup of flour and blend again on ① until the dough is smooth. Clean the sides of the pitcher. Add the remaining flour and pulse on ① until a smooth ball forms. Use a spatula to clean the sides of the pitcher and continue pulsing on ① for 2 minutes, or until the ball of dough is very smooth and elastic.

Place the dough in a lightly-oiled bowl, cover, and let rise for 60 minutes, or until doubled in size. Prepare a 9-inch by 5-inch loaf pan by lightly coating with cooking spray. Form the dough into a loaf shape and place in the loaf pan. Cover and let rise again for 45 minutes, or until doubled in size again.

Bake at 375°F for 35 to 40 minutes, or until the bread is golden brown. Cool on a wire rack before slicing.

WHOLE GRAIN COWBOY BREAD
Makes 1 loaf

Saddle up and enjoy the texture and flavors of this satisfying bread!

¼ CUP YELLOW CORN MEAL
¼ CUP DARK BROWN SUGAR, PACKED
1 TEASPOON SALT
1 CUP WATER, HEATED TO BOILING TEMPERATURE
2 TABLESPOONS CANOLA OIL
¼ OUNCE PKG. DRY ACTIVE YEAST
¼ CUP WATER, WARMED TO 110-115°F
⅓ CUP WHOLE WHEAT FLOUR
¼ CUP RYE FLOUR
2½ TO 3 CUPS WHITE FLOUR

Position the Dough Station as directed and insert the Dough Hook into the 40 oz. Pitcher. Place the corn meal, sugar, salt, 1 cup water, and oil in the pitcher and blend on ① for about 10 seconds. Remove from the pitcher and set aside. Let cool completely, about 30 minutes.

In a small bowl, dissolve the yeast in the warm water and stir well. Pour into the pitcher and add the cooled corn meal mixture. Add the whole wheat flour and the rye flour and blend on ① until smooth. Use a spatula to clean the sides of the pitcher. Add 1 cup of the white flour and blend again on ① until the dough is smooth and well-combined. Clean the sides of the pitcher. Add the remaining flour as needed and pulse for 2 minutes on ① until the dough is very smooth and elastic.

Form the dough into a round and place in a mixing bowl that has been lightly coated with cooking spray. Cover and let rise for 50 to 60 minutes, or until doubled. Punch down the dough and let rest for 5 minutes. Lightly coat a 9-inch by 5-inch loaf pan with cooking spray and shape the dough to fit into the pan. Cover and let rise for 30 to 45 minutes, or until doubled.

Preheat the oven to 375°F. Bake the bread for 35 to 45 minutes, or until the top is golden and the bread sounds hollow when tapped.

PARMESAN & DILL BISCUITS
Serves 6 to 8

Biscuits often highlight the sweeter side of breads and are served with honey or jam, however these savory dill and Parmesan cheese biscuits are less sweet and perfectly suited to accompany beef or chicken.

¾ CUP LOWFAT MILK

1 TEASPOON SALT

¼ CUP VEGETABLE SHORTENING

2 CUPS ALL-PURPOSE FLOUR

1 TABLESPOON BAKING POWDER

2 TABLESPOONS PARMESAN CHEESE, GRATED

1 TABLESPOON FRESH DILL, MINCED

Position the Dough Station as directed and insert the Dough Hook into the 40 oz. Pitcher. Place the milk, salt and shortening in the pitcher and blend until smooth. Add 1 cup of the flour and blend on ① until smooth. Clean the sides of the pitcher with a spatula and add the remaining 1 cup flour, baking powder, cheese and dill. Pulse on ① for 30 seconds. Clean the sides of the pitcher and pulse briefly again, just until the ingredients are incorporated.

Place the biscuit dough on a lightly floured board and gently round up. Pat the dough lightly with your hands into ½-inch thickness. Do not overwork the dough. Use a biscuit cutter to cut 12 to 16 biscuits. Gather the leftover dough together (without kneading) and cut additional biscuits.

Lightly coat a 9-inch x 9-inch baking pan with cooking spray and place the biscuits in the pan. The biscuits should touch each other and have little space between. Bake at 450°F for 10 to 12 minutes, or until fluffy and cooked through.

ITALIAN BREADSTICK TWISTS
Makes 32 bread sticks

Use any combination of spices on these breadsticks – you can't go wrong with any savory, zesty or spicy pairing.

¾ CUP LOWFAT MILK
1 TABLESPOON SUGAR
1 TEASPOON SALT
2 TABLESPOONS VEGETABLE OIL
¼ OZ. PKG. DRY ACTIVE YEAST
¼ CUP WATER, WARMED TO 115°F
3 TO 3½ CUPS ALL-PURPOSE FLOUR
1 EGG WHITE
1 TABLESPOON WATER
3 TABLESPOONS KOSHER SALT
1 TABLESPOON CRACKED BLACK PEPPER
1 TABLESPOON SESAME SEEDS
1 TABLESPOON POPPY SEEDS

Position the Dough Station as directed and insert the Dough Hook into the 40 oz. Pitcher. Place the milk, sugar, salt and oil in the pitcher and blend on ❶ for 10 seconds. Dissolve the yeast in the warm water and stir well. Add the yeast mixture to the pitcher.

Add 1 cup of the flour to the pitcher and blend on ❶ until the dough is smooth. Clean the sides of the pitcher with a plastic spatula and add 1 cup of flour. Blend on ❶ until smooth. Clean the sides of the pitcher again. Add the remaining flour as needed and pulse on ❶ for about 2 minutes, cleaning the sides of the pitcher as needed.

Turn the dough into a lightly oiled bowl and cover. Let rise until doubled, about 45 to 60 minutes.

Place the dough on a lightly floured board and roll into a 16-inch by 6-inch rectangle. From the widest side, cut ½-inch wide strips. Twist each strip by hand and place on a baking sheet that has been coated with cooking spray. Cover and let rise for 30 to 45 minutes.

In a small bowl, combine the egg white and water. Brush onto each breadstick. Scatter the salt, pepper and seeds over the breadsticks before baking. Bake at 400°F for 10 to 15 minutes. Cool slightly on a wire rack.

APRICOT & DATE MUFFINS

Makes 12 muffins

Made with dried dates and apricots, these muffins are naturally sweet and contain only 2 tablespoons of sugar! Add a little whipped butter for a brunch specialty.

1 CUP DATES
½ CUP DRIED APRICOTS
¾ CUP MILK
1 LARGE EGG
½ CUP VEGETABLE SHORTENING
2 TABLESPOONS SUGAR
2 CUPS ALL-PURPOSE FLOUR
2½ TEASPOONS BAKING POWDER
1 TEASPOON SALT

Place the dates and apricots in the 40 oz. Pitcher and blend on ② to uniformly chop. Remove and set aside.

Position the Dough Station as directed and insert the Dough Paddle into the 40 oz. Pitcher. Place the milk, egg, shortening and sugar in the pitcher and blend on ① until well-combined. Add 1 cup of the flour, the powder and the salt and blend on ① for about 10 seconds. Clean the sides of the pitcher with a spatula and add the remaining flour. Blend on ① for 10 seconds. Add the date/apricot mixture and pulse on ① until the dried fruit is incorporated throughout.

Prepare a 12-cup muffin tin by generously coating each cup with shortening or using foil liners. Scoop a large tablespoon of batter into each of the cups and divide the remaining batter evenly among all the cups.

Bake at 400°F for 25 minutes, or until baked through.

BANANA NUT BREAD
Makes 1 loaf

A classic bread for the holidays or any day you want a welcome treat with your hot coffee or tea. Some cooks prefer to cool this bread completely and cut into thin slices before serving with butter or cream cheese.

3 SMALL VERY RIPE BANANAS, PEELED
1 TABLESPOON LEMON JUICE
½ CUP BUTTER
¾ CUP SUGAR
2 EGGS
½ CUP MILK (AS NEEDED)
2 CUPS ALL-PURPOSE FLOUR
1½ TEASPOONS BAKING POWDER
½ TEASPOON SALT
½ TEASPOON BAKING SODA
¼ CUP WALNUTS

Position the Dough Station as directed and insert the Dough Paddle into the 40 oz. Pitcher. Place the bananas in the pitcher and blend on ❶ until smooth. Add the lemon juice, butter, sugar, eggs and almost all of the milk. Blend on ❶ until smooth. Add 1 cup of the flour, baking powder, salt and soda and blend on ❶ for about 10 seconds. Clean the sides of the pitcher and add more milk if needed. Add the walnuts and pulse again briefly.

Lightly coat a 9-inch by 5-inch loaf baking pan with cooking spray. Spoon the batter into the loaf pan and use a knife to evenly spread across the pan. Bake at 350°F for 1 hour, or until the loaf is cooked through and golden brown. Cool on a wire rack.

PECAN CINNAMON ROLLS

Makes about 8 to 9 rolls

These short-cut "one-rise" rolls are perfect for Saturday morning cooks who want to prepare and bake rolls quickly. The aroma of fresh baked rolls will delight the entire household.

¼ OZ. PKG. DRY ACTIVE YEAST
¼ CUP WATER, WARMED TO 110-115°F
⅔ CUP BUTTERMILK
1 LARGE EGG
¼ CUP BUTTER, MELTED
¼ CUP SUGAR
2¾ CUPS ALL-PURPOSE FLOUR
1 TEASPOON BAKING POWDER
1 TEASPOON SALT

BUTTERY PECAN CRUMBLE
¼ CUP BUTTER
1 TEASPOON GROUND CINNAMON
¼ CUP BROWN SUGAR, PACKED
½ CUP PECANS

Position the Dough Station as directed and insert the Dough Paddle into the 40 oz. Pitcher. Dissolve the yeast in the water and stir well. Pour into the pitcher. Add the buttermilk, egg, butter and sugar and blend on ❶ until smooth. Clean the sides of the pitcher with a spatula and add 1 cup of the flour, the baking powder and salt. Blend on ❶ for 30 seconds. Add the remaining flour and pulse to blend on ❶ for about 2 minutes, or until the ingredients are well-incorporated. Place the dough on a floured board. Clean the pitcher and dry.

Place the butter, cinnamon, brown sugar and pecans into the pitcher and blend on ❶ until uniformly chopped.

Roll the dough into a 12-inch by 7-inch rectangle and sprinkle the pecan butter mixture over the dough. Roll up the dough, beginning at the wide end. Pinch the long edge of the dough to seal. Cut into 12 slices and place in a lightly oiled 9-inch round baking pan. Let rise until doubled, about 60 to 75 minutes.

Bake at 375°F for 25 minutes. Remove and cool the rolls on a wire rack.

DOUBLE LEMON GLAZED CAKE

Makes 1 cake

Tart and tangy, best served in thin slices with crème fraiche or ice cream.

6 TABLESPOONS BUTTER
¾ CUP SUGAR
2 LARGE EGGS
ZEST OF 1 LEMON (RESERVE LEMON JUICE)
½ CUP LOWFAT MILK
1½ CUPS ALL-PURPOSE FLOUR
¼ TEASPOON SALT
1 TEASPOON BAKING POWDER

LEMON GLAZE
½ CUP SUGAR
JUICE OF ONE LEMON

Position the Dough Station as directed and insert the Dough Paddle into the 40 oz. Pitcher. Place the butter, sugar, eggs, lemon and milk in the pitcher and blend on ① until very smooth. Use a spatula to clean the sides of the pitcher if needed. Add the flour, salt and baking powder and blend on ① until the batter is smooth again.

Prepare a 9-inch by 5-inch loaf pan by coating with cooking spray. Pour the batter into the prepared pan and bake at 350°F for 1 hour.

As the lemon cake is baking, prepare the glaze by combining the sugar and juice in a small bowl. As soon as the cake is removed from the oven, pour the glaze over the cake. Place the pan on a wire rack to cool. When cool, remove the loaf and slice or refrigerate until use.

CINNAMON & NUTMEG SPICE DONUTS

Makes 8 to 9 donuts

Yummy! Dust one of these cake donuts with powdered sugar or eat just as they are, crispy, warm and sweet.

2 EGGS
1 TEASPOON VANILLA EXTRACT
½ CUP SUGAR
2 TABLESPOONS BUTTER
½ CUP MILK
2½ CUPS ALL-PURPOSE FLOUR
1½ TEASPOONS BAKING POWDER
½ TEASPOON SALT
¼ TEASPOON GROUND CINNAMON
¼ TEASPOON GROUND NUTMEG
OIL FOR FRYING
POWDERED SUGAR FOR GARNISH

Position the Dough Station as directed and insert the Dough Paddle into the 40 oz. Pitcher. Place the eggs, extract, sugar, butter and milk in the pitcher and blend on ❶ until smooth. Clean the sides of the pitcher with a spatula and add 1 cup of the flour, the baking powder, salt, cinnamon and nutmeg. Blend on ❶ for 30 seconds. Add the remaining flour and pulse on ❶ until the dough is smooth and well-incorporated.

Place the dough on a lightly floured board and roll into a ½-inch thickness. Cut with a donut cutter.

Choose a deep pan that will hold 3 inches of oil and heat on medium-high heat until 375°F (or use a deep fryer as directed). When the oil is ready, use a slotted spoon to place 3 to 4 donuts in the oil and fry for about 2 minutes. Turn and continue frying for 1 minute, or until both sides are crispy and brown and the donuts are cooked through. Repeat with the remaining donuts and donut holes, if desired. Dust with powdered sugar, if desired.

FRESH BLUEBERRY LEMON SCONES
Makes 16

Scones aren't meant to be light and flaky; they are considered to be a cross between a muffin and bread, so this makes scones perfect for brunch or teatime. Fresh blueberries add antioxidant power to your scones.

¾ CUP BUTTER
1 CUP BUTTERMILK
1 TEASPOON LEMON EXTRACT
½ CUP SUGAR
3 CUPS ALL-PURPOSE FLOUR
2½ TEASPOONS BAKING POWDER
½ TEASPOON BAKING SODA
1 CUP FRESH BLUEBERRIES, RINSED
SUGAR FOR DUSTING

Position the Dough Station as directed and insert the Dough Paddle into the 40 oz. Pitcher. Preheat the oven to 425*F. Place the butter, buttermilk, extract and sugar in the pitcher and blend on ① until very smooth. Add 1 cup of the flour, the baking powder and baking soda and blend again on ① until smooth. Use a spatula to clean the sides of the pitcher as needed. Add 1 cup of flour and blend on ① for about 10 seconds. Add the remaining flour and pulse on ① for about 10 seconds, or until the dough is uniform. Remove the dough paddle and lightly fold in the blueberries.

Divide the dough in half on a lightly floured board and pat each half into an 8-inch circle about ½-inch thick. Sprinkle each circle with sugar. Lightly press the sugar into the dough. Cut each round into 8 wedges using a sharp knife. Place the scones on a baking sheet about ½-inch apart and bake for 15 to 18 minutes. Serve while warm.

BLUEBERRY MUFFINS

Makes about 12 muffins

Super easy and super delicious! Serve while warm with sweet butter.

¾ CUP WHOLE MILK

1 LARGE EGG

½ CUP VEGETABLE SHORTENING

2 TABLESPOONS SUGAR

¾ TEASPOON SALT

2½ TEASPOONS BAKING POWDER

2 CUPS ALL-PURPOSE FLOUR

1 CUP FRESH BLUEBERRIES

Position the Dough Station as directed and insert the Dough Paddle into the 40 oz. Pitcher. Place the milk, egg, shortening and sugar in the pitcher and blend on ① until smooth. Add the salt, baking powder, and flour and blend on ① just until the ingredients are combined. Do not over-process. Remove the batter and fold in the blueberries.

Prepare a 12-cup muffin tin by coating each cup with cooking spray or lining each cup with foil or paper cups. Spoon the batter evenly into the muffin cups. Bake at 400°F for about 25 minutes, or until golden brown.

CHOCOLATE CHUNK MUFFINS

Makes 12 muffins

Rich, dark and moist, these muffins could almost be labeled "brownies" instead. You decide!

2 CUPS SEMI-SWEET CHOCOLATE CHIPS

¼ CUP BUTTER

4 LARGE EGGS

¾ CUP SUGAR

1 TEASPOON VANILLA EXTRACT

½ TEASPOON SALT

1 CUP ALL-PURPOSE FLOUR

1 CUP DARK CHOCOLATE CHIPS

½ CUP WALNUTS

½ CUP SEMI-SWEET CHOCOLATE CHIPS

Place the 2 cups chocolate chips and the butter in a medium microwave-safe bowl and heat for 1 minute. Stir and microwave again for 1 minute. Stir and repeat until the chips are melted and the mixture is smooth. Cool slightly. Position the Dough Station as directed and insert the Dough Paddle into the 40 oz. Pitcher. Spoon the chocolate and butter into the pitcher.

Add the eggs, sugar, vanilla, salt and flour. Blend on ❶ until smooth, cleaning the sides of the pitcher with a spatula, if needed. Remove the batter from the pitcher and add the dark chocolate chips to the batter. Stir to mix well.

Spoon the muffin batter into muffin cups that have been prepared with cupcake or foil liners.

Insert the blade in the 40 oz. pitcher and add the walnuts and remaining chocolate chips. Blend on ❸ until uniformly chopped. Sprinkle the chopped nut and chocolate mixture over the top of each muffin.

Bake at 350°F for 30 to 40 minutes, or until baked through. Cool on a wire rack.

CRANBERRY, ORANGE & WALNUT BREAD

Serves 8

A welcoming bread at breakfast or snack time. Best when served at room temperature with a schmear of cream cheese or butter.

1 FRESH ORANGE, PEELED, SECTIONED, SEEDS REMOVED

⅓ - ½ CUP MILK

¼ CUP BUTTER

1 CUP SUGAR

1 LARGE EGG

2 CUPS FLOUR

½ TEASPOON BAKING SODA

½ TEASPOON BAKING POWDER

½ TEASPOON SALT

½ CUP DRIED CRANBERRIES

½ CUP WALNUTS, CHOPPED

Place the orange sections in the 40 oz. Pitcher and blend on ② until fairly smooth. Strain the juice and discard the solids. Add enough milk to the juice to equal ¾ cup. Place the juice/milk mixture in the pitcher and add the butter, sugar and egg. Blend on ① for 10 seconds.

Position the Dough Station as directed and insert the Dough Paddle into the 40 oz. Pitcher. Add the juice mixture, butter, sugar and egg. Blend on ① for 10 seconds. Add 1 cup of the flour, the baking soda and powder and salt and blend on ① until smooth. Clean the sides of the pitcher with a spatula and add the remaining flour, blending on ① until just combined. Remove the batter and fold in the cranberries and walnuts by hand.

Lightly coat a 9-inch by 5-inch loaf pan with cooking spray and spoon the batter into the pan. Bake at 350°F for 50-60 minutes, or until the bread is baked throughout.

CHICKEN
FETTUCINI
ALFREDO
P. 137

CHAPTER EIGHT

ENTRÉES, SALADS & SIDES

SAUSAGE & ROASTED VEGETABLE PENNE PASTA

Makes 4 to 6 servings

4 ZUCCHINI, HALVED LENGTHWISE AND CUT INTO
1 INCH PIECES

2 MEDIUM ONIONS, PEELED AND QUARTERED

6 LARGE CLOVES GARLIC, PEELED

6 RIPE ROMA TOMATOES, CORED AND QUARTERED
LENGTHWISE

1 BULB FENNEL, TRIMMED AND CUT INTO
1 INCH PIECES

¼ CUP + 1 TABLESPOON EXTRA-VIRGIN OLIVE OIL

1 TEASPOON SALT

1 TEASPOON FRESHLY GROUND BLACK PEPPER

4 LARGE PRE-COOKED CHICKEN PESTO SAUSAGES,
SLICED INTO 1 INCH PIECES

16 OUNCE PKG PENNE PASTA, UNCOOKED

1 CUP CHICKEN STOCK

½ CUP WHITE WINE

2 TABLESPOONS FRESH BASIL LEAVES, CHOPPED

1 TABLESPOON FRESH OREGANO, CHOPPED

½ CUP PARMESAN CHEESE, FRESHLY GRATED

Preheat the oven to 400°F degrees. Place the zucchini, onions, garlic, tomatoes, and fennel in a large mixing bowl and toss with ¼ cup olive oil, salt and pepper. Arrange the vegetables loosely on 2 baking sheets lined with parchment paper; do not crowd. Roast vegetables for 15 to 20 minutes. Vegetables will be soft and slightly browned when done.

While the vegetables are roasting, brown the pre-cooked sausage in a large skillet in 1 tablespoon of olive oil. Prepare the penne pasta according to package directions. When the pasta is done, drain in a colander, retaining a few cups of pasta water. Keep the pasta warm by placing the colander over a bowl of the retained warm pasta water.

Place half of each type of roasted vegetable, in batches, into the 72 oz. Pitcher. Pulse on ① into a rough sauce, transferring each processed batch to the empty pasta stockpot. To the last batch, add chicken stock, wine, basil and oregano and process on ① until blended. Add to the vegetables in stockpot, set heat to medium-low and stir in the remaining un-blended roasted vegetables and chicken sausage.Thin the sauce, if desired, with additional chicken stock or water. Place the pasta in large serving bowl, add the sauce and toss. Garnish with the Parmesan cheese.

CHICKEN FETTUCCINI ALFREDO
Makes 4 servings

Your guests will never know how simple it was to create this stylish and sumptuous dish. A simple green salad and crusty French bread complete the scene.

2 TABLESPOONS EXTRA-VIRGIN OLIVE OIL
2 SKINLESS, BONELESS CHICKEN BREAST HALVES,
CUT INTO 1 INCH PIECES
½ TEASPOON SALT
1 TEASPOON FRESHLY GROUND BLACK PEPPER
16 OUNCE PKG. FETTUCCINI NOODLES,UNCOOKED
½ CUP UNSALTED BUTTER
2 CUPS HEAVY CREAM
1½ CUPS + ½ CUP PARMESAN CHEESE,
FRESHLY GRATED
1 TEASPOON FRESHLY GROUND BLACK PEPPER
4 TABLESPOONS FRESH FLAT-LEAF ITALIAN
PARSLEY, CHOPPED

In a large skillet, heat the oil over medium-high heat. Add the chicken, sprinkle with salt and pepper and sauté, stirring frequently, until lightly browned on all sides and cooked through. Do not crowd the pan, cook in batches if necessary.

Prepare the fettuccini according to package directions. When the pasta is done, drain in a colander, retaining a few cups of pasta water. Keep the pasta warm by placing a colander over a bowl of the retained pasta water.

Melt the butter in small sauce pan over low heat or in a microwave. Pour the heavy cream, melted butter and 1½ cups grated cheese into the 72 oz. Pitcher and blend on ❶ until smooth. Do not over mix. Transfer to a large sauté pan over low heat and cook, stirring frequently. When the sauce is hot and thickening, add the cooked fettuccini and chicken, gently tossing to coat with the sauce. Serve garnished with chopped parsley and the remainder of the Parmesan cheese.

BAKED TOMATILLO CHICKEN
Serves 4

A memorable dish from a super simple "made from scratch" salsa. The chicken is almost poached in the sauce and is so tender you can cut it with a fork. Make extra and serve the tomatillo "salsa" with chips!

1 POUND FRESH TOMATILLOS
1 LARGE WHITE ONION, PEELED AND CUT INTO CHUNKS
3 CLOVES GARLIC, PEELED
1 SERRANO CHILE PEPPER
½ PACKED CUP CILANTRO LEAVES
½ TEASPOON SALT
1 LARGE LIME, JUICED (ABOUT 2 TABLESPOONS)
4 SKINLESS, BONELESS CHICKEN BREAST HALVES

Remove the husks from the tomatillos and wash under running water until the tomatillos are no longer sticky. Cut each into quarters. Place into the 72 oz. Pitcher and add the onion, garlic and Serrano pepper and pulse on ① until roughly chopped. Add the cilantro, salt and lime juice and continue blending until the mixture is well-combined.

Preheat the oven to 350°F degrees. Place the chicken breasts in a baking dish and cover with the tomatillo sauce. Cover with foil and bake for 20 minutes. Remove the foil and continue baking for 5 to 10 minutes longer or until the chicken is cooked through and no pink remains.

PORK CHOPS WITH PROVENCE PRUNE SAUCE

Serves 2

Browning and baking in the same pan saves time and clean-up! This luscious sauce cooks into the pork giving it and elegant flavor. Spoon the sauce over the pork chops and add baked fingerling potatoes.

10 PRUNES, PITTED AND ROUGHLY CHOPPED
½ CUP BRANDY
½ CUP CHICKEN STOCK
2 TEASPOONS DRIED SAGE
3 PIECES APPLE SMOKED BACON, CHOPPED
2 SHALLOTS, PEELED AND FINELY CHOPPED
2 BONELESS PORK CHOPS, EACH 1½ INCH THICK
1 TABLESPOON EXTRA-VIRGIN OLIVE OIL
½ TEASPOON FRESHLY GROUND BLACK PEPPER

Place prunes and brandy in a small saucepan over medium heat and cook until small bubbles begin to form at the sides, reduce the heat to low and simmer for 20 minutes, until the prunes are softened. Place half of the prune/brandy mixture into the 72 oz. Pitcher and add the chicken stock and sage. Blend on ❷ until the mixture is smooth. Preheat the oven to 350°F degrees. In an oven-proof skillet, sauté the bacon and shallots over medium-high heat until the shallots begin to caramelize and the bacon is crispy. Using a slotted spoon, remove the bacon/shallot mixture, leaving some of the drippings, and set aside.

Pat the pork chops dry and lightly rub both sides with olive oil and sprinkle with pepper. Return the skillet to medium-high heat; add the pork chops when the pan is hot and brown on both sides. Reduce the heat to medium, return the shallots and bacon to pan, add the pureed prune sauce and remaining chopped prunes with the brandy. Place the skillet in the oven, cover with foil and bake for 30 to 40 minutes, or until the chops are 150°F internally. Allow the meat to rest for a few minutes before serving. Spoon any remaining sauce over the chops and serve.

MINI CRAB RAMEKINS

Serves 4

With all the flavors of Maryland crab cakes, this is easy to do ahead. Serve with a salad of field greens and mild, sweet dinner rolls.

8 SLICES STALE OR DAY OLD WHITE BREAD, CRUSTS REMOVED

¼ CUP UNSALTED BUTTER

1 CUP REGULAR OR LOWFAT MAYONNAISE

2 TEASPOONS DIJON MUSTARD

1½ TEASPOONS WORCESTERSHIRE SAUCE

2 EGGS, LIGHTLY BEATEN

2 TEASPOONS CHESAPEAKE BAY STYLE SEAFOOD SEASONING

2 6 OUNCE CANS LUMP CRABMEAT, DRAINED (OR 12 TO 16 OUNCES FRESH CRABMEAT)

2 MEDIUM SHALLOTS, MINCED

2 MEDIUM INSIDE RIBS OF CELERY, WITH LEAVES, WASHED, TOUGH STRINGS REMOVED, MINCED

1 TEASPOON FRESH LEMON JUICE

1 TABLESPOON FRESH PARSLEY, CHOPPED

1 TEASPOON FRESHLY GROUND BLACK PEPPER

Preheat the oven to 350°F degrees. Cut the bread into large pieces, place into the 72 oz. Pitcher and pulse on ① until the bread is completely crumbled. Melt the butter in a small saucepan over low heat or in a microwave, mix with the bread crumbs and set aside.

Place the mayonnaise, mustard, Worcestershire sauce, eggs, and seafood seasoning in the pitcher and blend on ② until well-combined. Pick through crabmeat and remove any cartilage or shell fragments and add to the mixture along with all remaining ingredients, reserving ½ of the buttered bread crumbs. Pulse on ① to combine. Divide the mixture among buttered individual ramekins and top with the remaining buttered bread crumbs.

Bake for 25 to 30 minutes until the tops are golden brown and the crab casseroles are piping hot. Serve warm with garnishes of lemon juice, parsley and black pepper. Add a crusty French bread to round out this entrée.

SMOKED PAPRIKA CHICKEN PASTA IN SWEET RED PEPPER SAUCE

Makes 6 to 8 servings

Smoky sweet paprika defines this luscious entrée.

3 RED BELL PEPPERS, SEEDED AND
COARSELY CHOPPED
3 CLOVES GARLIC, PEELED
1 MEDIUM WHITE ONION, PEELED AND
QUARTERED
¼ CUP TOASTED PINE NUTS
2 TEASPOONS SMOKED PAPRIKA, DIVIDED
1½ TEASPOON SALT, DIVIDED
1½ TEASPOON FRESHLY GROUND BLACK PEPPER,
DIVIDED
½ CUP WHITE FLOUR
2 TABLESPOONS CANOLA OIL
4 BONELESS, SKINLESS, CHICKEN BREASTS, CUBED
1 CUP CHICKEN STOCK
½ CUP HEAVY CREAM
2 ZUCCHINI, HALVED LENGTHWISE AND CUT INTO
1 INCH PIECES
½ CUP PARSLEY, CHOPPED
16 OUNCE PKG RIGATONI PASTA, UNCOOKED
½ CUP PARMESAN CHEESE, FRESHLY GRATED

Place the bell peppers, garlic, onion, pine nuts, 1 teaspoon smoked paprika, ½ teaspoon salt and ½ teaspoon black pepper into the 72 oz. Pitcher and blend on ① into a rough, but uniform pulp.

Place the flour, 1 teaspoon each of salt, pepper and paprika in self-sealing plastic bag. Add the chicken pieces in batches, shaking to coat with the flour. Heat 2 tablespoons of oil in a large skillet over medium-high heat. When the oil is hot, fry the chicken until golden brown on all sides and cooked through, with no pink remaining. Do not crowd the pan; cook in batches if needed. Remove the fried chicken and keep warm.

Clean the skillet and add the blender sauce, stock, cream, zucchini and parsley. Heat on medium and cook for 10 to 15 minutes, stirring often. Add the chicken and adjust the seasonings, if desired. Prepare the rigatoni according to package directions. When the pasta is done, drain and place in a large shallow serving bowl, add the sauce and toss to mix well. Garnish the pasta with freshly grated Parmesan cheese.

SPAGHETTI MARINARA

Makes 3 cups sauce - Enough for 4 to 6 servings

Fresh and simple flavors create a fast classic that is as healthy as it is flavorful. The olive oil adds richness but may be omitted with good results for a lower fat version of this sauce. Use as a pasta sauce, or to create dishes such as chicken parmesan or baked lasagna. Freezes well for up to 2 months.

28 OUNCE CAN WHOLE PEELED TOMATOES, WITH JUICE FROM CAN
¼ CUP TIGHTLY PACKED FRESH BASIL LEAVES
½ MEDIUM YELLOW ONION, PEELED AND QUARTERED
3 CLOVES GARLIC, PEELED
½ CUP WATER
½ CUP GOOD RED WINE
½ TEASPOON SALT
½ TEASPOON FRESHLY GROUND BLACK PEPPER
1 TABLESPOON EXTRA-VIRGIN OLIVE OIL
16 OUNCE PKG SPAGHETTI NOODLES, UNCOOKED
½ CUP PARMESAN CHEESE, FRESHLY GRATED

Place all of the ingredients except the olive oil, spaghetti noodles and Parmesan cheese into the 72 oz. Pitcher and blend on ❷ until the vegetables are finely chopped and the sauce is semi-smooth. In a large skillet, heat the oil over medium heat. Add the sauce from the blender, stir to incorporate the oil, reduce the heat to low and simmer the sauce, partially covered, for 15 minutes.

Prepare the spaghetti according to package directions. When the pasta is done, drain in a colander, and transfer the cooked pasta to a large serving bowl. Pour the sauce over the pasta and toss gently to coat. Top with the Parmesan cheese just before serving.

CREAMY SCALLOPED POTATOES
Makes 4 to 6 servings

The *Ninja™ Kitchen System* takes the work out of making a smooth cream sauce. Add your favorite cheese and butter to make this quick cheese sauce that spreads over tender potatoes. Yum!

1 CUP WHOLE MILK
1 CUP HEAVY CREAM
1 TABLESPOON FRESH THYME LEAVES
½ TEASPOON GROUND NUTMEG
4 TABLESPOONS WHITE FLOUR
4 TABLESPOONS SOFTENED BUTTER
2 POUNDS RUSSET POTATOES, PEELED AND CUT INTO 1/8-INCH THICK SLICES
PINCH SALT
PINCH FRESHLY GROUND BLACK PEPPER
1 CUP PARMESAN CHEESE, GRATED

Preheat the oven to 375°F degrees. Place the milk, cream, thyme, nutmeg and flour into the 72 oz. Pitcher and blend on ② until smooth. Transfer to a saucepan, and cook on medium heat, stirring constantly until the mixture is slightly thickened, about 5 minutes. Butter a 9-inch by 11-inch baking dish. Place a layer of potato slices in the pan in an overlapping pattern and sprinkle with salt and pepper. Remove the sauce from the heat and pour one-third of the sauce over the potatoes. Top with ¼ cup Parmesan cheese.

Repeat this process, creating 2 layers, ending with a final dusting of Parmesan cheese. Add more cheese to top, if desired. Bake, uncovered, for 45 minutes until the top is golden brown and slightly crunchy and the potatoes are cooked through and semi-blended with the sauce.

MIDDLE EASTERN TABOULI
Serves 6

A traditional Middle Eastern dish made with bulgur wheat, which is found in the bulk food or Ethnic Food section at your local grocery store. A great dish to make when you have extra tomatoes or lemons that need to be used.

1 CUP PLAIN BULGUR (CRACKED WHEAT), UNCOOKED
1 CUP WATER
1 BUNCH FRESH PARSLEY, STEMMED
6 SPRIGS FRESH MINT, STEMMED
½ SMALL WHITE ONION, PEELED
2 CLOVES GARLIC, PEELED
⅓ CUP EXTRA VIRGIN OLIVE OIL
2 LEMONS, JUICED (ABOUT ¼ CUP)
½ TEASPOON SALT
½ TEASPOON FRESHLY GROUND BLACK PEPPER
2 RIPE TOMATOES, CORED AND DICED
3 GREEN ONIONS, CLEANED AND CHOPPED

In a large bowl, mix the bulgur with the water. Cover and let stand for 20 minutes, until the water is absorbed and the wheat is tender.

Place the parsley, mint, onion and garlic into the 40 oz. Pitcher and pulse on ① to make a small, rough chop, cleaning the sides of the pitcher with a spatula as necessary. Transfer the mixture to the bowl of softened bulgur.

Place the olive oil, lemon juice, salt and pepper in the pitcher and blend on ① until incorporated. Add the dressing to the bulgur mixture and lightly toss to mix. Add the chopped tomatoes and green onion, again tossing gently to mix. Taste and adjust the seasonings. Serve well-chilled or at room temperature.

CAESAR SALAD WITH GARLIC CROUTONS

Serves 4

CAESAR SALAD DRESSING

2 LARGE EGG YOLKS

2 TEASPOONS WORCESTERSHIRE SAUCE

3 LARGE LEMONS, JUICED (6 TABLESPOONS)

2 CLOVES GARLIC, PEELED

½ TEASPOON SALT

1 TEASPOON FRESHLY GROUND BLACK PEPPER

8 ANCHOVY FILLETS OR 3 TEASPOONS ANCHOVY PASTE

2 TEASPOONS DIJON MUSTARD

⅔ CUP EXTRA-VIRGIN OLIVE OIL

⅔ CUP PARMESAN CHEESE, GRATED

FOR CROUTONS AND SALAD

2 LARGE CLOVES GARLIC, PEELED AND MINCED

¼ CUP EXTRA-VIRGIN OLIVE OIL

1 SMALL FRENCH BAGUETTE, CUT INTO 1 INCH CUPS

4 HEARTS ROMAINE LETTUCE, TORN INTO SMALL PIECES

FRESHLY SHAVED PARMESAN CHEESE, FOR TOPPING

Place the egg yolks, Worcestershire sauce, lemon juice, 2 cloves garlic, salt, pepper, anchovy fillets or paste and mustard into the 72 oz. Pitcher and blend on ② until the mixture is very smooth. With the blender running, slowly pour two-thirds cup olive oil through the top pouring tab in a steady stream to emulsify the dressing. Add the Parmesan cheese and pulse on ① to blend. Cover and refrigerate until ready to use.

Preheat the oven to 350°F degrees. Combine 2 cloves of the minced garlic, ¼ cup oil, and bread cups in a bowl and toss to coat. Spread the bread cups onto a baking sheet and bake, watching carefully, until golden brown, about 10 minutes.

To assemble the salads, place the torn lettuce in a large bowl, toss with the dressing and top with the croutons and shaved Parmesan cheese. Serve at once.

TANGY SUMMER FRUIT SALAD

Makes 4 to 6 servings

Sweetened fruit topped with a dollop of tart yogurt is the perfect refresher on a hot summer day.

1 CUP TIGHTLY PACKED FRESH MINT LEAVES
⅓ CUP SUPERFINE SUGAR
1 POUND FRESH STRAWBERRIES,
CLEANED, HULLED AND HALVED
1 POUND FRESH BLACKBERRIES,
CLEANED AND DRIED
3 FIRM-RIPE PEACHES OR NECTARINES,
PITTED, AND CUT INTO CHUNKS
1 MEDIUM HONEYDEW MELON, HALVED,
SEEDED AND CUT INTO BITE-SIZED CHUNKS
1 CUP GREEK YOGURT

Place the mint leaves and sugar into the 72 oz. Pitcher and blend on ❶ until finely ground. Mix the fruit in a large serving bowl and toss with the desired amount of minted sugar. Serve in individual bowls topped with a dollop of Greek yogurt.

Tip

What's the difference between typical plain yogurt and Greek yogurt? Greek yogurt is thicker and more rich-tasting than plain yogurt. It is often higher in protein and lower in sugar than plain yogurt.

BLT SALAD
WITH BLUE CHEESE DRESSING

Makes about 2 cups dressing - Enough salad for 4

This classic salad is like a BLT without the bread! A firm and heavy head of iceberg makes a superior salad. It's worth taking the time in the market to find just the right one.

4 OUNCES GOOD QUALITY BLUE CHEESE
½ CUP REGULAR MAYONNAISE
½ CUP SOUR CREAM
½ CUP BUTTERMILK
1 TABLESPOON TARRAGON VINEGAR
½ TEASPOON SALT
½ TEASPOON FRESHLY GROUND BLACK PEPPER
1 FIRM HEAD ICEBERG LETTUCE, CUT INTO
4 LARGE WEDGES
1 RIPE TOMATO, SLICED
1 CUP FRESH BACON CRUMBLES

Place the Blue cheese, mayonnaise, sour cream, buttermilk, vinegar, salt and pepper into the 40 oz. Pitcher and blend on ① until smooth.

Place a wedge of iceberg lettuce on each serving plate. Pour one-fourth of the dressing on each of the lettuce wedges, place tomato slices on the side and top with bacon crumbles.

BALSAMIC & STRAWBERRY VINAIGRETTE

Makes about 1 1/4 cups

A rich and sweet vinaigrette that dresses up any salad. Try tossing dried cranberries, toasted pecans and apples with field greens to give this dressing a boost!

¼ CUP FRESH STRAWBERRIES, HULLED AND CHOPPED
1 TABLESPOON STRAWBERRY JAM
¼ TEASPOON SALT
⅛ TEASPOON FRESHLY GROUND BLACK PEPPER
2 TABLESPOONS BALSAMIC VINEGAR
¾ CUP EXTRA VIRGIN OLIVE OIL

Place the strawberries, jam, salt, pepper and vinegar into the 40 oz. Pitcher and blend on ❶ until very smooth. With the blender running, slowly pour the olive oil through the top pour tab in a steady stream to emulsify the dressing. Taste and adjust the flavors.

☀ Tip

This dressing quickly becomes a sumptuous summer sauce when heated slightly and brushed over fish or chicken while grilling.

APPLE, CRANBERRY & GORGONZOLA SALAD

Serves 4

Refreshing and appealing! Perfect when serving fish or chicken as your entrée.

2 LARGE FUJI APPLES, CORED AND ROUGHLY CHOPPED
1 MEDIUM CUCUMBER, PEELED AND ROUGHLY CUT
½ CUP WALNUTS, HALVED
1 CUP DRIED CRANBERRIES
½ CUP GORGONZOLA CHEESE, CRUMBLED
½ CUP SOUR CREAM
¼ CUP CREAM CHEESE
2 TABLESPOONS MILK
PINCH SALT
PINCH BLACK PEPPER
1 LARGE CUCUMBER, THINLY SLICED HORIZONTALLY

Place the apples in the 72 oz. Pitcher and blend on ① until chopped. Remove the apples and place in a mixing bowl. Place the cucumber and walnuts in the pitcher. Blend on ① for a few seconds until roughly chopped. Remove and add to the apples. Add the dried cranberries and toss. Set aside.

Place the cheese, sour cream, cream cheese, milk, salt and pepper in the pitcher. Blend on ① until mostly smooth. Remove and set aside.

To serve, form the long slices of cucumber into circular shapes and use a wooden pick to secure. Place each on a salad plate. Fill the cucumber cups with the apple, cucumber mixture and top each salad with the gorgonzola salad dressing.

KANSAS CITY
BARBECUE SAUCE
P. 158

CHAPTER NINE

MARINADES, RUBS & MOPPING SAUCES

TERIYAKI GRILLING MARINADE

Makes about 2 cups

After removing the meat from this marinade, pour the marinade into a saucepan, bring to a boil, and simmer for 5 minutes, making a luscious sauce for your grilled masterpiece.

2 CLOVES GARLIC, PEELED
2 TABLESPOONS FRESH GINGER, PEELED AND ROUGHLY CHOPPED
¼ WHITE ONION, PEELED
¼ CUP FRESH CILANTRO, STEMMED
¾ CUP SOY SAUCE
½ CUP RICE WINE VINEGAR
2 TEASPOONS ASIAN CHILE PASTE
1 TABLESPOON HONEY
2 TABLESPOONS FRESH LIME JUICE
¾ TEASPOON TOASTED SESAME OIL

Place the garlic, ginger, onion and cilantro into the 72 oz. Pitcher and pulse on ② until uniformly chopped. Add the remaining ingredients and blend on ② until mixed well, but with a slightly chunky consistency. Add a little chicken stock or water to thin, if desired.

❋ Tip

Pour this marinade into a self-sealing plastic bag and add a 1½ pound beef flank steak. Seal and marinate for 24 hours. Remove the steak, pat dry and grill for about 8 minutes per side over medium-high heat. Let rest for 5 minutes, then slice thinly across the grain. The result? Perfectly tender and flavorful teriyaki steak!

SMOKING CHIPOTLE SAUCE

Makes about 1 cup

A chipotle is a dried, smoked jalapeño pepper with a spicy, smoky, slightly sweet flavor. It is often canned in a vinegary sauce called adobo. Add chipotles to stews, soups, sauces and salsas. Use it sparingly until you determine how much "fire" you want to add to your favorite foods!

3 CHIPOTLES, CANNED IN ADOBO SAUCE, OR LESS IF A MILDER SAUCE IS DESIRED

1 TABLESPOON ADOBO SAUCE FROM CANNED CHIPOTLES

4 CLOVES GARLIC, PEELED

2 ORANGES, PEELED AND PULLED INTO QUARTERS

1 LIME, JUICED

1 TABLESPOON TOMATO PASTE

2 TABLESPOONS APPLE CIDER VINEGAR

1 TABLESPOON EXTRA VIRGIN OLIVE OIL

1 TEASPOON GROUND CUMIN (OR MORE TO TASTE)

1 TEASPOON MEXICAN OREGANO

½ TEASPOON SALT

½ TEASPOON FRESHLY GROUND BLACK PEPPER

Place all ingredients into the 72 oz. Pitcher and blend on ❷ until smooth. Transfer to a medium sauce pan, over medium heat and bring to a boil. Reduce the heat to medium-low and simmer, stirring frequently, for 5 to 10 minutes. Thin with a little water if necessary. Cover and store in the refrigerator until use.

✳ Tip

All of the citrus acid in this recipe – oranges, lime, and apple cider vinegar – combine to tenderize meat perfectly. You can use this sauce alongside your favorite grilled meat, or pour the sauce into a self-sealing plastic bag with beef, chicken or pork before grilling and marinate it for a few hours.

LEMON & HERB MARINADE

Makes about 1 cup

This marinade also works beautifully as a tangy fresh salad dressing.

2 LEMONS, JUICED (4 TO 6 TABLESPOONS)
¾ CUP EXTRA-VIRGIN OLIVE OIL
1 TABLESPOON FRESH THYME LEAVES
1 SMALL SPRIG FRESH PARSLEY
1 SMALL PIECE FRESH OREGANO
½ TEASPOON SALT
½ TEASPOON FRESHLY GROUND BLACK PEPPER

Place all ingredients into the 72 oz. Pitcher and blend on ❷ until smooth. Taste and adjust the flavors to your liking. Use right away or cover and store in the refrigerator. If chilled, let stand at room temperature for 10 minutes to allow the oil to liquefy before serving.

Tip

Makes a light marinade for white fish fillets. Marinate the fish in the refrigerator for no more than one hour. Broil or grill and serve with lemon slices.

ORANGE PAPAYA SHRIMP MARINADE

Serves 4 to 6

A fruity marinade with a spicy Asian twist. Serve fabulous char-grilled shrimp over a bed of aromatic jasmine rice.

1 MEDIUM PAPAYA, PEELED AND QUARTERED

1 MEDIUM ORANGE, PEELED AND
PULLED INTO QUARTERS

2 LIMES, JUICED

2 GREEN ONIONS, CLEANED, ROOT END REMOVED

2 TABLESPOONS FRESH BASIL LEAVES

¾ CUP SOY SAUCE

1 CUP WATER

2 TABLESPOONS HONEY

½ TEASPOON FIVE SPICE POWDER (OR MORE
TO TASTE)

2 POUNDS FRESH SHRIMP, DEVEINED AND
CLEANED, TAILS REMOVED

Pulse the papaya and orange in the 72 oz. Pitcher on ❶ until roughly chopped. Add the remaining ingredients, except the shrimp, and blend on ❸ until the marinade is well combined and semi-smooth. Taste and adjust the flavors and consistency, if desired. Pour the marinade over the shrimp in a self-sealing plastic bag. Seal and refrigerate for at least 30 minutes or longer for a more intense flavor. Discard the marinade and place the shrimp on skewers. Grill the shrimp skewers for about 3 minutes per side. Makes about 1½ cups marinade.

KANSAS CITY BBQ SAUCE

Makes about 3 cups

Kansas City, Missouri is considered by many to be the barbeque capitol of America. No wonder with over 100 barbecue restaurants in the city!

1 CUP KETCHUP
¼ CUP APPLE CIDER VINEGAR
¼ MEDIUM WHITE ONION, PEELED
2 CLOVES GARLIC, PEELED
1 CUP TOMATO SAUCE
¼ CUP BROWN SUGAR, PACKED
2 TABLESPOONS MOLASSES
2 TABLESPOONS FRESH LEMON JUICE
1½ TEASPOONS SMOKED PAPRIKA
1 TEASPOON FRESHLY GROUND BLACK PEPPER
½ TEASPOON RED CHILE POWDER
½ TEASPOON SALT

Place the ketchup, vinegar, onion and garlic into the 72 oz. Pitcher and blend on ① until smooth. Add the remaining ingredients and continue blending on ② until the sauce is semi-smooth.

Transfer the sauce to a medium saucepan and simmer, stirring occasionally, over low heat for 20 minutes, or until the sauce reduces by one-third. Cover and store in the refrigerator.

✳ Tip

For smoking, for grilling, for marinating, for barbeque beans – this sauce does it all!

SWEET PAPRIKA RUB
Makes 3/4 cup

A fragrant and flavorful dry rub for a roast chicken or turkey that also creates tasty drippings for gravy.

½ CUP FIRMLY PACKED BROWN SUGAR
2 TABLESPOONS SWEET PAPRIKA
2 TEASPOONS ONION POWDER
2 TEASPOONS DRY MUSTARD
1 TEASPOON CRUSHED RED PEPPER
½ TEASPOON SALT
½ TEASPOON GARLIC POWDER
½ TEASPOON CELERY SEED

Place all ingredients into the 72 oz. Pitcher and pulse on ❶ for 10 seconds, until the spices and sugar are well combined. Use right away or store in an airtight pitcher, in a dark, dry area, for up to 6 months.

Tip
Smoked Hungarian sweet paprika is a specialty food item, however you can usually find it in kitchen shops, or in the ethnic food aisle of your grocery store. You can also order it easily online from various outlets. Sweet paprika opens up an entirely new flavor dimension versus the tinned ground paprika we typically use. Once you try sweet paprika, you'll probably never reach for that old tin again.

GREEK HERB RUB

Makes 1 3/4 cups

Bring the Mediterranean into your kitchen with this very aromatic rub! It is wonderful on all meats and fish, and especially on roast lamb.

½ CUP DRIED GREEK OREGANO
½ CUP DRIED THYME
¼ CUP DRIED PARSLEY
¼ CUP DRIED MARJORAM
1 TABLESPOON DRIED DILL (OPTIONAL)
1 TEASPOON FRESHLY GROUND BLACK PEPPER
½ TEASPOON SALT
¼ CUP EXTRA VIRGIN OLIVE OIL

Place all ingredients, except the olive oil, into the 72 oz. Pitcher and pulse on ❶ for 10 to 20 seconds. Transfer the herbs to a mixing bowl, add oil and toss to just coat the spices. Use right away or store in an airtight pitcher, in a dark, dry area, for up to 6 months.

Tip

It's best to let this rub sit for at least 6 to 8 hours before using. This will allow the flavors to marry into each other and the oil will be better absorbed. Slather it over any cut prior to grilling for a fabulous treat.

COWBOY MOPPING SAUCE

Makes about 2 cups

A thinner sauce than most marinades or barbeque sauces, mopping sauce got its name from the small slathering "mops" used for basting the meat during cooking. The purpose of a mopping sauce is to keep meat moist and add flavor during grilling. Due to the low sugar content it is not prone to burn.

¼ SMALL WHITE ONION, PEELED

2 CLOVES FRESH GARLIC, PEELED

½ CUP WHITE WINE VINEGAR

12 OUNCE CAN REGULAR BEER, NOT LIGHT

1 LEMON, JUICED

2 TEASPOONS DIJON MUSTARD

½ TEASPOON FRESHLY GROUND BLACK PEPPER

½ TEASPOON SALT

½ TEASPOON GROUND PAPRIKA

½ TEASPOON CAYENNE PEPPER

Place the onion, garlic and vinegar into the 72 oz. Pitcher and blend on ②, cleaning the pitcher with a spatula as needed, until finely chopped. Add the remaining ingredients and continue processing until smooth. Use right away or cover and store in refrigerator.

❋ Tip

Perfect for guys who like the thrill of the grill, this sauce is great for multiple bastings as the meat cooks. Use it liberally!

BALSAMIC GRILLING SAUCE

Makes about 1 1/2 cups

This delicious sauce will create a tasty char on grilled meat.

2 TABLESPOONS OLIVE OIL
1 LARGE SHALLOT, PEELED AND MINCED
1 CUP BALSAMIC VINEGAR
¾ CUP KETCHUP
2 TABLESPOONS BROWN SUGAR
1 TABLESPOON GARLIC MUSTARD
½ TEASPOON SALT
½ TEASPOON FRESHLY GROUND BLACK PEPPER

Heat the oil in a small saucepan over medium heat; add the shallot and sauté, stirring frequently. When fragrant and soft, add the remaining ingredients, stirring well to combine. Reduce the heat to low and simmer for 10 to 15 minutes. Remove and let stand until completely cool. Transfer the sauce to the 72 oz. Pitcher and blend on ② until smooth. Use or cover and store in refrigerator.

Tip

Substitute small sweet onions or green onions if you don't have shallots on hand. The onion flavor blends well with the distinctive balsamic vinegar in this special sauce.

FRESH FIG SAUCE

Makes about 1 1/2 cups

A classic combination, fresh figs and balsamic vinegar, produce an extraordinary topping for grilled meats or sumptuous desserts. There is nothing like fresh figs, but dried figs substitute beautifully if fresh are not available.

10 FRESH OR DRIED BLACK MISSION FIGS
½ CUP BALSAMIC VINEGAR
⅓ CUP WHITE WINE
⅓ CUP BRANDY
¼ CUP ORANGE JUICE
¾ CUP WATER
2 TABLESPOONS HONEY
½ TEASPOON GROUND CARDAMOM (OPTIONAL)
¼ CUP BUTTER

Wash and de-stem the figs if using fresh fruit. Place all of the ingredients, except the butter, into the 72 oz. Pitcher and blend on ① until the sauce is smooth.

In a small sauce pan, melt the butter over medium-low heat. Add the fig sauce from the blender and bring just to a boil. Reduce the heat to low and simmer, stirring frequently, until the sauce thickens, about 20 minutes. Use at once or cover and store in the refrigerator.

Tip

This outrageously wonderful sauce is great when first made when served warm with goat cheese over toasted baguette slices. But, it is even better when stored in the refrigerator for 24 hours and slathered cold over scones or muffins for a special morning treat!

CRANBERRY & ORANGE RELISH

Makes about 4 cups

This relish is so delish you will want to use it year around! If fresh cranberries are unavailable, use frozen. For variety, add cinnamon, vanilla or a splash of orange liqueur.

1 MEDIUM ORANGE, PEELED AND PULLED INTO QUARTERS
12 OUNCE BAG FRESH CRANBERRIES
1 TABLESPOON SUGAR, OR TO TASTE
1 TABLESPOON ORANGE LIQUEUR (OPTIONAL)

Place all ingredients into the 72 oz. Pitcher and blend on ❷ until finely chopped and uniform. Taste and add more sugar, if desired. Transfer to a storage bowl, cover and chill for at least two hours, allowing the flavors to marry.

Tip

You can only imagine how wonderful this relish tastes when combined with chicken or turkey! Try smoothing this relish on whole wheat bread and adding turkey slices, blue cheese crumbles and arugula for an out-of-this-world sandwich.

CHOCOLATE CHIP
MINT ICE CREAM
P. 170

CHAPTER TEN

DESSERTS & SWEET TREATS

EASY NEW YORK CHEESECAKE
Serves 6

Using a few shortcuts, such as a prepared graham cracker crust and your *Ninja™ Kitchen System*, makes preparing this cheesecake a breeze.

8 OUNCES CREAM CHEESE, SOFTENED
½ CUP SUGAR
2 TABLESPOONS LEMON JUICE
1 TEASPOON VANILLA EXTRACT
PINCH SALT
2 LARGE EGGS
8 INCH PREPARED GRAHAM CRACKER CRUST

1 CUP SOUR CREAM
2 TABLESPOONS SUGAR
½ TEASPOON VANILLA EXTRACT

Place the cream cheese, sugar, lemon juice, extract, salt and eggs in the 72 oz. Pitcher and blend on ② until smooth. Use a spatula to clean the sides of the pitcher and blend again on ② for 30 seconds. Pour the filling into the prepared crust and smooth the top.

Bake at 325°F for 20 minutes. If not set in the center, continue baking for 5-7 minutes or until the center is set. Meanwhile, in a small bowl, combine the sour cream, sugar and vanilla and mix until smooth. Spoon over the top of the cheesecake and continue baking for 10 minutes. Remove from the oven and cool on a wire rack. Refrigerate when cool. Refrigerate any leftovers after serving.

Tip
Top with canned cherries, blueberries or fresh strawberries and cream for the perfect accent to the creamy cheesecake.

ROCKY ROAD FUDGE PIE

Serves 8 to 10

Whip together peanuts, marshmallows and chocolate chips make this a stand-out dessert.

1 CUP MINI MARSHMALLOWS
½ CUP ROASTED PEANUTS
½ CUP SEMI-SWEET CHOCOLATE CHIPS
16 OUNCES CREAM CHEESE, SOFTENED
¼ CUP SUGAR
½ CUP LOWFAT MILK
2½ CUPS PREPARED WHIPPED CREAM (OR WHIPPED TOPPING)
8-INCH PREPARED CHOCOLATE CRUMB PIE CRUST
½ CUP DARK FUDGE SAUCE

Place the marshmallows, peanuts and chocolate chips in the 72 oz. Pitcher pitcher and pulse on ① to uniformly chop. Remove and place in a large mixing bowl. Place the cream cheese, sugar and milk in the pitcher. Blend on ② until very smooth and add the mixture to the chopped marshmallows, peanuts and chips in the mixing bowl. Add the whipped cream and fold in lightly to incorporate. Spoon the pie mixture into the pie crust and smooth evenly over the top.

Freeze for 4 to 6 hours or until set. Before serving, drizzle the dark fudge sauce over the pie. Cut into 8 to 10 pieces and serve right away. Refrigerate or freeze leftovers.

CHOCOLATE CHIP MINT ICE CREAM

Makes 3 to 4 servings

Peppermint flavor and chocolate chips adorn this rich ice cream. Fill a 1½ to 2 quart ice cream maker for best results.

2½ CUPS HEAVY CREAM
1 CUP SEMI-SWEET CHOCOLATE CHIPS
2 TABLESPOONS SUGAR
1 TEASPOON PEPPERMINT EXTRACT
FEW DROPS GREEN FOOD COLORING, OPTIONAL

Place the cream, chocolate chips, sugar, peppermint extract and food coloring in the 72 oz. Pitcher. Blend on ❷ for about 10 seconds. Pour the ice cream mixture into the freezer bowl or tub of your ice cream maker and proceed as directed.

PEACHES & CREAM ICE CREAM
Makes about 3 1/2 quarts

Use ripe peaches for the best flavor and texture and get ready to receive the compliments! This recipe can be used with a 5 or 6 quart ice cream freezer.

5 FRESH, RIPE PEACHES, PEELED AND PITTED
6 LARGE EGGS
2½ CUPS SUGAR, DIVIDED
2 TABLESPOONS CORNSTARCH
1 TABLESPOON VANILLA EXTRACT
PINCH SALT
4 CUPS WHOLE MILK
3 CUPS HEAVY CREAM

Place the peaches in the 72 oz. Pitcher and blend on ② until uniformly smooth. Remove the peaches and chill in the refrigerator.

Clean the pitcher and dry. Place the eggs, sugar, cornstarch, vanilla and salt in the 72 oz. Pitcher and blend on ② until smooth.

In a large saucepan, heat the milk and cream until steaming. Do not boil. Pour about one-half cup of milk and cream mixture into the egg mixture and blend on ① for 10 seconds. Remove the egg mixture from the pitcher and slowly add to the hot milk and cream mixture in the pan, stirring as the two are slowly combined.

Bring the mixture to a very low simmer and stir for about 3 minutes, until smooth and thick. Remove from the heat and chill for several hours.

Just before pouring the cream into the freezer, add the peaches and stir by hand. Pour the ice cream mixture into the freezer and proceed as directed.

VANILLA BEAN ICE CREAM

Makes about 3 quarts

Grind whole vanilla beans quickly in your *Ninja™ Kitchen System* and add to this ice cream for authentic flavor. This recipe will fill a 5-quart freezer.

4 WHOLE VANILLA BEANS
2½ CUPS WHOLE MILK
2½ CUPS SUGAR
½ TEASPOON SALT
2½ CUPS LIGHT CREAM
1 TABLESPOON VANILLA EXTRACT
5 CUPS HEAVY CREAM

Place the vanilla beans in the 72 oz. Pitcher and pulse on ❶ until the beans are fairly ground. Remove the beans and set aside. Clean the blender and dry.

In a large saucepan, scald the whole milk. Remove from the heat and cool. Pour the milk into the 72 oz. Pitcher and add the sugar, salt and light cream. Blend on ❷ until very smooth. Pour into a large mixing bowl and add the extract and heavy cream. Stir lightly and add the ground vanilla beans.

Refrigerate the ice cream mixture for 1 hour, then pack and freeze as directed.

FROZEN CHOCOLATE FUDGE YOGURT

Serves 2 to 3

Perfectly chocolately and smooth – made for two! Use with a 1½ or 2 quart ice cream maker.

¾ CUP SUGAR
2 TEASPOONS CORNSTARCH
12 OUNCE CAN EVAPORATED MILK (MAY SUBSTITUTE LOWFAT)
1 TEASPOON VANILLA EXTRACT
6 OUNCES CHOCOLATE YOGURT
¼ CUP CHOCOLATE FUDGE SAUCE

In a medium saucepan over medium heat, combine the sugar and cornstarch. Stir and add the milk until the mixture begins to steam. Continue cooking and stirring as you add the milk. Continue stirring until the mixture is slightly thickened and smooth. Remove from the heat. Chill for 4 hours in the refrigerator.

Place the vanilla extract and chocolate yogurt in the 72 oz. Pitcher and add the fudge sauce. Blend on ❶ until smooth. Slowly pour the cream mixture into the chocolate sauce and blend on ❸ until very smooth.

Pour the chocolate yogurt into an ice cream bowl or tub and freeze as directed.

LEMON MINT GRANITA

Serves 4

Very simple and oh, so satisfying on a hot summer day. Using your *Ninja™ Kitchen System* eliminates the need to stir the frozen mixture every 30 minutes, making this the easiest dessert of all.

3 LARGE LEMONS, PEELED
4 LEAVES FRESH MINT, WASHED
1 CUP WATER
⅓ SUPERFINE SUGAR (YOU MAY ALSO USE REGULAR SUGAR)
MINT FOR GARNISH, IF DESIRED

Place the lemons, mint leaves and water in the 72 oz. Pitcher and blend on ❸ until very smooth. Strain all of the juice through a sieve and discard the fruit.

Pour the juice into a bowl or tray. Cover and freeze for 3 to 4 hours, or until almost completely frozen. Remove the ice from the bowl and place in the pitcher. Process on ❸ for 30 seconds, or until the granita is fluffy and uniform. Spoon or pour into 4 small glasses and serve with a spoon at once. Garnish with mint sprigs before serving, if desired.

WATERMELON GRANITA

Serves 4 to 5

Cool, refreshing and a wonderful way to use the ripe watermelon sitting in your refrigerator. You may store the granita for up to 1 month in your freezer before processing in your *Ninja™ Kitchen System*. Cover tightly during storage.

6 CUPS RIPE WATERMELON, PEELED AND SEEDED, ROUGHLY CUT
1 TABLESPOON LIME JUICE
1½ CUPS SUPERFINE SUGAR (YOU MAY ALSO USE REGULAR SUGAR)

Place the watermelon chunks in the 72 oz. Pitcher in one or two batches, if needed and blend on ① for 1 minute. Remove the fruit and strain through a sieve. You should have about 5 cups of juice. Discard the fruit and return the juice to the blender.

Add the lime juice and sugar and blend on ② to thoroughly combine the ingredients. Pour the juice into a bowl or ice cube trays and freeze until almost solid, about 3 to 4 hours.

Just before serving, place the iced juice in the pitcher and process on ③ for 30 seconds. The granita should be somewhat smooth and a little slushy. Pour into small glasses and serve at once.

CRISP & RICH BUTTER COOKIES

Makes about 6 dozen cookies

Use a cookie press to create any shapes you want, from bars and stars to hearts and candy canes.

1 CUP BUTTER
½ CUP SUGAR
PINCH SALT
1 LARGE EGG
1 TEASPOON VANILLA EXTRACT (SUBSTITUTE LEMON EXTRACT)
½ TEASPOON ALMOND EXTRACT
2½ CUPS ALL-PURPOSE FLOUR

Position the Dough Station as directed and place the Dough Paddle in the 40 oz. Pitcher. Place the butter in the pitcher. Blend on ① until very light and fluffy. Add the flour and pulse on ① until combined. Remove the dough paddle and clean the sides of the pitcher with a spatula, mixing in any unblended dough. Cover with the lid and chill the dough for about 20 minutes.

Fill a cookie press and press shapes onto ungreased cookie sheets. Bake at 400°F for 8 to 10 minutes. Cookies should be set, but not browned, when done. Cool on wire racks before serving.

Tip

If your cookie dough is too soft to press, pop the dough into the refrigerator to chill for at least 30 minutes. Remove only enough dough to fill the press and keep the remaining amount chilled until filling the press.

CARAMEL OATMEAL BARS

Makes 14 to 16 bars

Filled with gooey caramel, these enticing oat and nut bars will satisfy your craving for chewy and soft, savory and sweet.

⅔ CUP BUTTER, SOFTENED
1 CUP DARK BROWN SUGAR, PACKED
1 CUP + 3 TABLESPOONS FLOUR
1¼ CUPS QUICK-COOKING OATS
¾ CUP WALNUTS, CHOPPED
12 OUNCE JAR CARAMEL TOPPING
(OR CARAMEL SAUCE)

Preheat the oven to 350°F. Grease and flour a 9-inch by 9-inch baking pan.

Position the Dough Station as directed and place the Dough Paddle in the 40 oz. Pitcher. Place the butter in the pitcher and add the sugar. Blend on ❶ until creamy. Add 1 cup of the flour and the oats and pulse on ❶ until well-combined. Use a spatula to clean the sides of the pitcher, if needed.

Press one-half of the mixture into the prepared pan and bake for 10 minutes. Remove from the heat and sprinkle with the walnuts. In a small bowl, mix together the caramel and 3 tablespoons flour. Pour over the nuts and top with the remaining oat mixture.

Bake for 20 to 25 minutes and cool on a rack before serving. Refrigerate for about 1 hour before serving to make cutting the bars a little bit easier.

ENGLISH TOFFEE COOKIES

Makes about 24 cookies

Thin and crisp, with a chocolate and almond candy coating!

1 CUP BUTTER, SOFTENED
½ CUP DARK BROWN SUGAR, PACKED
½ CUP SUGAR
1 TEASPOON VANILLA EXTRACT
1 EGG YOLK
2 CUPS CAKE FLOUR
PINCH SALT
10 OUNCE MILK CHOCOLATE CANDY BAR, MELTED
½ CUP ALMONDS, CHOPPED

Position the Dough Station as directed and place the Dough Paddle in the 40 oz. Pitcher. Place the butter, sugars, extract and egg yolk in the pitcher and blend on ❶ until smooth and creamy. Use a spatula to clean the sides of the pitcher. Add 1 cup of flour and salt. Blend on ❶ again until smooth. Add the remaining flour and pulse on ❶ until smooth.

Spoon the cookie dough onto a baking sheet that has been coated with cooking spray. Allow a 2-inch margin, as the dough will spread.

Lightly spread the chocolate over the dough and sprinkle the nuts over all. Bake at 350°F for 15 to 20 minutes. Cool slightly and cut into small squares. Cool on a wire rack.

SOFT MOLASSES DROPS

Makes about 3 dozen

Full of a warm molasses and sugar flavor with just a hint of ginger and cloves!

¾ CUP BUTTER
1 CUP DARK BROWN SUGAR, PACKED
1 EGG
¼ CUP DARK MOLASSES
2¼ CUPS FLOUR
2 TEASPOONS BAKING SODA
¼ TEASPOON SALT
½ TEASPOON CLOVES
1 TEASPOON GROUND CINNAMON
1 TEASPOON GROUND GINGER
GRANULATED SUGAR FOR GARNISH

Preheat the oven to 375*F. Position the Dough Station as directed and place the Dough Paddle in the 40 oz. Pitcher. Place the butter, brown sugar, egg and molasses in the pitcher and blend on ① until smooth. Place 1 cup of the flour and the remaining ingredients in the pitcher and blend on ① until well-combined. Clean the sides of the pitcher with a spatula as needed. Add the remaining flour and blend again until the flour is incorporated.

Drop the dough by teaspoons onto a baking sheet that has been lightly coated with cooking spray. Sprinkle each cookie with a few drops of water and sprinkle sugar over each cookie. Bake for 10 to 12 minutes, or until set. Cool on a wire rack and store tightly covered.

LEMON, COCONUT & WALNUT BARS

Makes about 24 bars

A wonderful sweet concoction of nutty and tart flavors! Cut these while slightly warm and serve warm or at room temperature. Yum!

½ CUP BUTTER
1½ CUPS DARK BROWN SUGAR, PACKED, DIVIDED
1 CUP ALL-PURPOSE FLOUR
2 LARGE EGGS
2 TABLESPOONS LEMON JUICE
ZEST 1 LEMON
½ TEASPOON SALT
1 CUP SHREDDED COCONUT
1 CUP WALNUTS, CHOPPED
½ CUP RAISINS

Preheat the oven to 350*F. Position the Dough Station as directed and place the Dough Paddle in the 40 oz. Pitcher. Place the butter, 1 cup of brown sugar and flour in the pitcher and blend on ① until crumbly and smooth. Press the mixture evenly into the bottom of an ungreased 9-inch by 13-inch baking pan. Bake for 10 minutes. Remove from the oven and set aside.

Place the remaining brown sugar, eggs, lemon juice, lemon zest and salt in the pitcher and blend on ① for about 20 seconds. Add the coconut, walnuts and raisins and blend on ① for 15 seconds. Pour or spoon the lemon and coconut topping over the flour and butter mixture and spread the topping evenly. Bake for 25 minutes, or until the topping is lightly browned. Cool for 10 minutes and cut into bars.

APPLESAUCE CAKE
WITH BUTTERCREAM FROSTING

Serves 8 to 10

Packed with juicy apples, nuts and raisins and crowned with fluffy sweet icing, this sublime cake will delight your senses.

2½ CUPS ALL-PURPOSE FLOUR
1½ CUPS SUGAR
¼ TEASPOON BAKING POWDER
1½ TEASPOONS BAKING SODA
1½ TEASPOONS SALT
1 TEASPOON GROUND CINNAMON
½ TEASPOON GROUND CLOVES
½ TEASPOON GROUND ALLSPICE
½ CUP SHORTENING
½ CUP WATER
1½ CUPS UNSWEETENED APPLESAUCE
2 MEDIUM EGGS
½ CUP WALNUTS, CHOPPED
1 CUP RAISINS

BUTTERCREAM FROSTING
¼ CUP BUTTER, SOFTENED
1¼ CUPS POWDERED SUGAR
½ TEASPOON VANILLA EXTRACT
PINCH SALT
2 TEASPOONS MILK

Preheat the oven to 350°F. Grease and flour a 9-inch by 13-inch baking pan. Position the Dough Station as directed and place the Dough Paddle in the 40 oz. Pitcher. Place the flour, sugar, baking powder, soda, salt, and spices in the pitcher and pulse on ❶ for 10 seconds. Add the shortening, water, applesauce and eggs and blend again on ❶ until smooth. Use a spatula to clean the sides of the pitcher if needed. Add the nuts and raisins and pulse on ❶, just until the walnuts and raisins are incorporated.

Pour the batter into the prepared pan. Bake for 50 to 60 minutes or until the center is firm. Remove and cool on a rack.

To prepare the frosting, place the butter, sugar, vanilla, salt and milk in the pitcher and blend on ❸ until the frosting is very smooth and fluffy. Frost the cooled cake and serve.

PINEAPPLE NUT CRUMB CAKE
Serves 8 to 10

This moist and delectable cake offers a twist on traditional pineapple upside-down cake. Pineapple slices and a rich crumbly cake take the top!

½ CUP BUTTER

¾ CUP SUGAR

2 EGGS

1½ TEASPOONS VANILLA EXTRACT

1¼ CUPS ALL-PURPOSE FLOUR

1 TEASPOON BAKING POWDER

1 FRESH PINEAPPLE, PEELED, CORED, QUARTERED LENGTHWISE AND SLICED

CRUMB TOPPING

1¼ CUPS ALL-PURPOSE FLOUR

½ CUP SUGAR

¼ TEASPOON GROUND CINNAMON

½ CUP BUTTER

½ CUP WALNUTS

Preheat the oven to 350°F. Butter the bottom and sides of a 10-inch springform pan. Position the Dough Station as directed and place the Dough Paddle in the 40 oz. Pitcher. Place the butter in the pitcher and blend on ① until very fluffy. Add the sugar and blend again on ① for 10 seconds. Use a spatula to clean the sides of the pitcher. Add the eggs and vanilla and blend on ① until uniformly smooth.

Add the flour and baking powder and blend on ① just until all the ingredients are moistened. Pour the batter into the prepared pan.

In the 40 oz. Pitcher, combine the flour, sugar and cinnamon for the crumb topping. Add the butter and walnuts and pulse on ① for 20 seconds. Remove and set aside.

Place the pineapple slices on top of the batter, leaving a ½-inch margin around the outside edge. Scatter the crumb mixture over the top. Bake for 50 to 60 minutes, or until the cake is firm.

Remove the cake and cool. Remove the pan rim and place on a serving platter.

KEY LIME PIE
Serves 6 to 8

Love the smooth and tart flavor of bright Key limes?
This is your dessert!

2 LARGE EGGS
14 OUNCE CAN SWEETENED CONDENSED MILK
4 KEY LIMES, JUICED TO EQUAL ½ CUP (YOU
MAY ALSO USE THE JUICE OF LIMES OR
BOTTLED LIME JUICE)
1 8-INCH PREPARED GRAHAM CRACKER CRUST
1 CUP WHIPPED CREAM

Preheat the oven to 350*F. Place the eggs in the 72 oz. Pitcher and blend **3** until light and frothy. Add the milk and lime juice and blend on **2** to incorporate.

Pour the batter into the graham cracker crust and bake for 10 minutes. Remove and cool. Chill for about 2 hours before serving. Serve with whipped cream.

*Tip

What makes key limes so special? Typical limes, or Persian limes, have a tart, yet somewhat smooth flavor. Key limes are much smaller and have a higher acidic acid and mouth-puckering tartness. As such, key limes are prized in sauces, marinades and, of course, key lime pie. If you can't find key limes in your grocery store, you may be able to find bottled key lime juice, or simply substitute Persian limes in equal proportions.